An Introduction to Lean Construction

Applying Lean to Construction Organizations and Processes

Larry Rubrich

WCM Associates LLC
Fort Wayne, IN
www.wcmfg.com

An Introduction to Lean Construction
Applying Lean to Construction Organizations and Processes

By
Larry Rubrich

Second Printing

WCM Associates LLC
834 Mill Lake Road
Fort Wayne, IN 46845
260-637-8064
Fax: 260-637-8071
www.wcmfg.com

Disclaimer

Demonstrations and illustrations contained herein provide only a description of general improvement techniques and methods. Illustrations and directions may not provide all necessary or relevant information, and the author suggests that you refer to appropriate equipment manuals specific to the particular task or contact a qualified craftsman or professional. By purchasing this book and not immediately returning it after reviewing this disclaimer, you agree that the author may not be held responsible for any omissions or inaccuracies in any information provided herein.

ISBN # 978-0-9793331-3-2

Book and text design by WCM Associates LLC
Book Cover designed by Kelly Fischer
Cover photo: ©iStockphoto.com/shotbydave

Printed and bound by:
Thomson-Shore, Inc.
Dexter, MI
734-426-3939

Library of Congress Control Number: 2012934981

Acknowledgments

To my wife, Shirley, who has supported me in my passion for Lean. Since my first book in 1998 (which was many years in the making), she has supported and tolerated my thousands of hours of writing. She has provided valuable book improvements during the layout, editing, and proofing processes. In Lean Team Building, we teach that producing the best information or physical product requires a diverse team whose members can look at the product from different angles or facets. Shirley's comments make everything I do better.

Vince Fayad, friend and partner at WCM Associates. Coauthor with me of the book *Policy Deployment and Lean Implementation Planning,* which is the basis of Chapter 2, and the four components of Lean, an expression and concept that Vince developed.

Lanner Fayad, Vince's son, was a Project Manager/Engineer for a mechanical contractor in Hawaii. Lanner provided some jobsite construction stories that, as Lanner described them, were "the kind of fire fighting that went on everyday" on projects. Lanner is now a Lean Facilitator.

Ted Angelo, an Executive Vice President at the Grunau Company, provided guidance and support for this book, including pictures, charts, and great feedback.

As an early adopter of Lean and Lean Construction activities (2003), Ted became a Lean Construction expert and developed the Lean Project Schedule (PS) shown in Chapter 5.

Ted is the author of the book *Lean Construction—One Company's Journey to Success,* published in the spring of 2012.

Rob Chartier, Director of Project Development at CG Schmidt in Milwaukee provided an initial review of the book outline, and his comments were beneficial in developing the scope and depth required in Chapters 4 and 5—the Lean Construction Tools.

As an "outside the box" thinker, Rob was able to help convert some of my crazy ideas into workable project tools and improvements.

Additionally, Rob provided feedback from a CM/GC view, which was valuable in translating some Lean Manufacturing tools and activities into workable Lean Construction actions.

Todd Henderson, an architect for Boulder Associates, Inc., and **Klaus Lemke**, VP of Milwaukee Operations for Miron Construction Co., Inc., deserve a special thanks. Their knowledge and experience in both Lean and Lean Construction and their well-written comments, brutally honest as necessary, improved the book considerably.

Gloria Garver, provided valuable assistance with the book layout and proofreading, curtailing my excessive use of *that* in my writing.

Kelly Fischer, my daughter, did the cover design, text layout, and coordination with the book printer (Thomson Shore) in her usual outstanding manner. This book could not exist without her.

In addition, the following individuals reviewed drafts of the book and provided very valuable feedback:

Nancy Burrows
Workforce Specialist
The Business & Career Institute
South Suburban College

Dr. Mark Federle
Associate Chair and Professor
Department of Civil, Construction and Environmental Engineering
Marquette University

Gary Kusnierz,
VP Performance Excellence
Affinity Health System

Kris Roberts
National Lean Manager
Turner Construction Company

Stephen Villarreal
Senior Risk & Process Improvement Manager
CF Jordan Construction

Table of Contents

About the Author

Larry Rubrich has over 35 years of experience in engineering and manufacturing in the automotive, industrial, and consumer products areas. He has held the positions of product engineer, chief product engineer, product manager, customer service manager, area manufacturing manager, continuous improvement manager, and general manager with Fortune 100 corporations.

Larry's passion for lean developed in 1987, when he spent time in Japan studying Japanese management and manufacturing techniques. He worked directly with a top-level Japanese consulting group hired by a U.S. company to implement the Toyota Production System (TPS) in its plants. Larry continued his commitment to implementing Lean by using Lean techniques to turn around facilities at Dana Corporation and United Technologies.

Larry is a registered Professional Engineer and founded WCM Associates LLC in 1997. WCM Associates LLC (www.wcmfg.com) is a business consulting, training, and publishing company dedicated to making American companies globally competitive through the implementation of Lean/World Class Enterprise. WCM Associates specializes in Lean Manufacturing, Lean Construction, Lean Healthcare, and Lean Service.

Larry and WCM Associates first began Lean Construction training in 2003 with Grunau Company, a Milwaukee based MEP subcontractor (Grunau is now a division of the API group). WCM Associates has completed Lean training at Willis A. Smith Construction, CenterPoint Engineering, CG Schmidt, Jamar Company, Tweet/Garot Mechanical and others.

Larry, along with Ted Angelo, co-presented "Using Lean Value Stream Mapping (VSM) in Support of Target Value Design" at the 2011 Lean Construction Institute (LCI) Congress meeting in Pasadena. In October, 2011, Larry presented "Sustaining Lean" to the LCI Chapter meeting held in Milwaukee.

Larry has written several widely acclaimed books on Lean, including:

√ *Implementing World Class Manufacturing*, co-authored with fellow associate, Mattie Watson.

√ *How to Prevent Lean Implementation Failures—10 Reasons Why Failures Occur.*

√ *Policy Deployment and Lean Implementation Planning—10 Step Roadmap to Successful Policy Deployment Using Lean as a System*, co-authored with fellow associate, Vince Fayad.

WCM Associates is also recognized for publishing other cutting-edge books on Lean, including the Shingo Prize winning Lean accounting book *Who's Counting? A Lean Accounting Novel*, by Jerry Solomon.

Foreword

This book is of tremendous value to any construction professional who has been exposed to Lean, to any companies that have already undertaken a Lean journey, or to those that are contemplating doing so. It is not a "magic tome" that provides all the answers, nor is it a full instruction manual detailing how your Lean journey will unfold. Instead, this book provides insight into what lies ahead of any company ready to commit to transformation into a World Class organization.

CG Schmidt, for whom I work, likes to describe itself as a provider of professional construction services—not a commodity builder. Given that identity, Lean Construction was of immediate appeal to the leaders of our organization.

Like many firms, we chose to embark on our Lean journey without the help of outside professionals. We read books. We attended seminars and conferences. We attempted several initiatives with varying levels of success. Ultimately, we discovered that, although our corporate culture was ready for the transformation, we still lacked a basic understanding; we lacked "system thinking."

Not to be dissuaded, we reached out to some of our Lean practicing clients and subcontractors. In doing so, we soon discovered a common denominator in their respective Lean journeys: Larry Rubrich.

As you explore Lean as a system of operation, you will find abundant information from which to draw, most of which is centered in manufacturing. Larry brings to the table a unique perspective, one that is pervasive in this book. While his background is in manufacturing, his thoughts and astute observations regarding Lean Construction go beyond the usual philosophy and instruction.

The Lean Construction Institute has emerged as the predominant voice of advocacy for Lean transformation within the construction industry. Naturally, other organizations (AGC, AIA) have embraced Lean as a school of thought as well. These groups have directed their messages toward optimizing construction at the project level. What sets this book apart—why it is truly unique—is its wholly organizational focus. It brings three concepts together (Policy Deployment, Core Lean Tools, and Lean Construction Tools) into one all encompassing culture. As Larry points out clearly in these pages, few organizations that merely implement Lean tools realize significant or sustained improvements. For a company to truly reinvent itself as a World Class organization, Lean must permeate and grow from within its very culture.

While Lean operating principles have been gathering the attention of American businesses since the 1980's, construction has yet to truly embrace the idea. Why has construction not yet come to realize that the way we deliver projects is an old, fragmented process? Is Lean the next evolution of the industry? Will Lean Construction, despite the current economic pressures to commoditize the delivery, come to thrive?

Based on what Larry shares within these pages, I don't know if we as constructors/buyers of construction services can afford not to take a serious look.

Robert H. Chartier, P.E.

Introduction

The purpose of this book is to provide the participants of Construction Industry processes with an overview of Lean Construction so they can eventually become a World Class organization. This is achieved through a successful implementation of Lean Construction as the "operating system" in their organization.

Lean Construction is about eliminating organizational waste to improve the flow of construction information and material. A better, faster flow of both information and material means construction projects that have higher quality, higher productivity (working smarter not harder) and are delivered with more owner value and shorter project lead times.

A successful Lean Construction implementation can occur only through the training, empowerment, and participation of the organization's entire workforce.

Origins of Lean Construction – The Lean Construction Institute (by Greg Howell)

"The Lean Construction Institute (LCI) was founded in 1997 to develop and disseminate new knowledge regarding the management of work in projects. The idea for an LCI developed from a discovery of the obvious; current project management practice cannot produce predictable workflow. This insight led to a reinterpretation of the source and nature of problems arising on construction projects. A new planning system, the Last Planner® System (LPS), was developed to improve workflow predictability. Taking advantage of the stability created by LPS, contractors, designers and suppliers began to organize and manage the work in projects as production systems. The development of Integrated Project Delivery grew from the realization in collaborative "Pull" planning sessions that the difficulty of moving money across contractual boundaries inhibited innovation.

From these beginnings, a group of academics, designers, contractors and construction owners worked together to extend and develop what is now called Lean Construction."

Does the Construction Industry Need Lean?

In the book, *Broken Buildings, Busted Budgets: How to Fix America's Trillion-Dollar Construction Industry*, author Barry LePatner explains that a survey of construction site productivity studies shows that 49.6% of jobsite time is spent on wasteful activities. Based on our experience, this number is understated due to the difficulty people have in defining owner value and waste when it is something they have done the same way for the past 15 years. This number probably approaches 75% when waste is correctly measured as "anything that does not provide value to the owner." Additionally, it is interesting to note that few people talk about administrative productivity. Again, based on our experience, typically 75% of the time spent in administrative tasks is waste. Very few companies have had the "this is value—this is waste" discovery session with their administrative staffs. Like manufacturing, our productivity problems are blamed on the hourly/trade associates when it is the "system" cost we should be worried about. We will discuss this further in Chapter 1.

In *The Owners Dilemma*, author Barbara White Bryson, an owner representing Rice University, comments on the entire building delivery system saying:

> Frankly, the inefficiency of the industry, whether in product delivery, construction technology, or design factors, is inexcusable and

amounts to billions of dollars of unnecessary waste paid for by public and private owners. This waste impacts design and construction projects by making them as much as 30 percent more expensive to build and maintain than necessary. This, in turn, discourages viable business plans, eats away at institutional endowments, reduces the aspirations of school districts, and raises taxes for communities wishing to fix roads and build community centers. In a $1 trillion industry, that amounts to as much as $300 billion of waste per year—of owner's money.

Additional support for the need for Lean in construction is shown in the following chart:

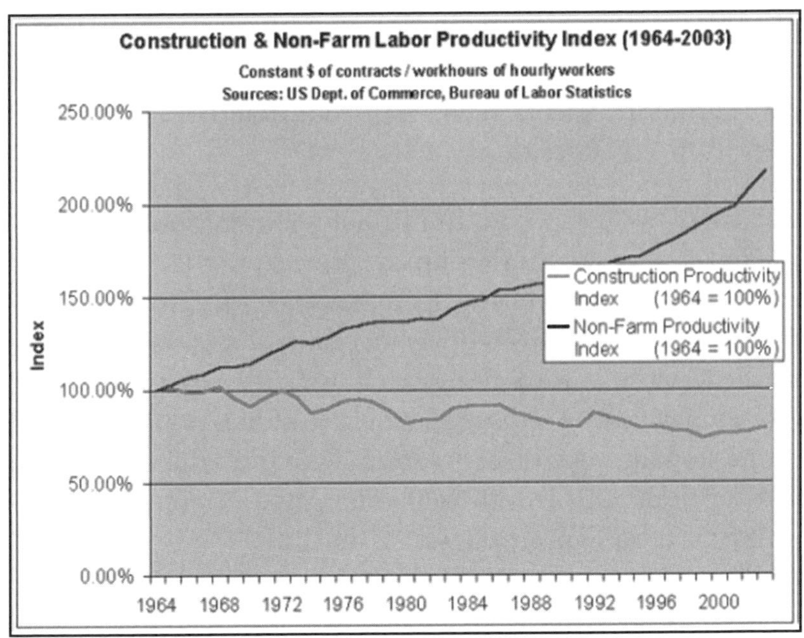

Construction Industry Productivity

This chart, the most recent data of this type from the U.S. Department of Commerce, shows that, while non-farm productivity (including manufacturing) has more than doubled since 1964, construction productivity has actually decreased. Because the positive increase in the non-farm productivity index has not stopped manufacturing from fleeing to foreign shores, the negative construction productivity growth may be spurring construction competitors to the United States. China Construction America, Inc., established in 1985 in New Jersey, now has five North American locations.

Fortunately, implementing Lean is not “rocket science,” so the chart on page 13 represents—and should be seen as—a great opportunity to improve.

However, Lean does require an organization’s Leadership Team to be firmly committed to Lean. Two of the many companies we were involved in exemplify that commitment. The first is from manufacturing, the second from construction.

For many readers, the manufacturing example will immediately appear not to apply. However, the reality is—and this understanding is necessary for the organization to be successful with Lean—business waste is business waste. When a manufacturing process stops flowing, waste is created; when a construction project stops flowing, waste is created. The only difference is in the types of waste and their amounts. (There are 8 general types, shown on pages 25 and 26.) Waste is waste—no industry is different.

As Shigeo Shingo, co-developer of the Toyota Production System on which Lean is based, said; “It doesn’t matter whether you are making automobiles or baking bread, waste is the same.”

Manufacturing Example – Improvements over Two Years

- Safety, from 32 lost-time accidents per year to 0 per year
- Productivity improvement = 90% (no capital expenditures)
- Financials, from loss to profitability ($586,0000 monthly turnaround)
- Union volunteered to decertify

Construction Example – Improvements over Three Years

- $279,000 total annual cost savings due to Lean process changes
- 5700 square feet reduction in required shop space
- 6% improvement in service productivity
- Offices consolidated within available space

Overview of Chapters

Chapter 1, *An Introduction to Lean*, continues the discussion of what waste is and how to identify it in a construction project, as well as how eliminating waste gives project participants an opportunity to supply more value to the owner.

In Chapter 2, *Planning the Lean Construction Implementation*, we note that improving the flow of information starts with the RFP, which dictates the use of Lean as an operating system. This operating-system approach is discussed in Chapter 2.

Lean as an operating system has four components:

- Lean Planning—the linking together of the organization's goals with the Lean activities to achieve those goals. This linking is called Policy Deployment.
- Lean Concepts—eliminating waste to improve the flow of information and material.
- Lean Tools—the techniques used to eliminate the identified waste.
- Lean Culture—building a positive working environment foundation for Lean through the use of leadership, communication, empowerment, and teamwork.

All four components must be implemented simultaneously as we will discuss in Chapter 2. The current construction industry discussion with its focus only on Lean Tools is a concern because we have learned through trial and experience that this limited focus is a serious mistake.

The fullest use of Lean's power of continuous improvement occurs only when organizations use Lean as a business strategy (Lean Planning) and as a way of running their organizations (Lean Culture) to achieve their business goals. To properly implement these two components, you must also understand the Lean Concepts and Lean Tools, which are the easy parts of the Lean Construction journey. Lean Concepts and Lean Tools can continuously improve the following construction results (assuming these results are part of your organization's goals):

- Safety
- Quality

- Productivity
- Project delivery

Simultaneously, Lean Concepts and Lean Tools can significantly reduce the following:

- Project lead times
- Project costs

The remainder of Chapter 2 explains how to complete the 10 Step Policy Deployment (PD) process necessary for implementing the Lean Planning component. That section is required reading for the Leadership Team (as defined at the end of this Introduction). Others may just skim or skip the PD section in Chapter 2.

It should be noted that PD is not something an organization does in addition to current budgeting and strategic planning processes. PD should be integrated into these processes. In smaller organizations, PD generally replaces the budgeting and strategic planning processes.

Chapter 3, *Developing a Lean Culture*, discusses the top management leadership requirements for Lean to be successful as a system implementation because the four components of Lean can be implemented only from the top. Addressing leadership requirements is part of developing the fourth component of Lean, a Lean Culture.

Because Lean can be fully implemented only through the training, empowerment, and participation of the entire workforce, Chapter 3 also discusses the development of empowerment and teamwork in the organization. This discussion includes how Lean thinking must permeate the organization, including the Human Resources area, in terms of associate behavioral expectations, associate evaluations, hiring, promotions, merit increases, and bonuses.

> At the management "report out" of a recent Kaizen Event (a team-based process improvement activity), a 30-year company employee told management how pleased he was at having the opportunity to participate in the event. "For 30 years the company has paid me to use my arms and my legs to do my job—and if they would have asked—they could have had my brain for free."

Chapter 4, *The Core Lean Tools*, identifies, defines, and gives examples of the Core Lean Tools used in all industries to eliminate the waste that is common to all. Again, the waste that is targeted for elimination is the waste that is preventing us from achieving our business goals as identified in Lean Planning and Policy Deployment.

Because the amount of waste (identified in Chapter 1) varies widely by industry, Lean is often broken into four industry categories: Lean Manufacturing, Lean Construction, Lean Healthcare, and Lean Service.

Chapter 5, *The Lean Construction Tools*, discusses the waste elimination tools that are primarily used in Lean Construction as a result of its "project" orientation. These tools include Integrated Project Delivery™ (IPD), Target Value Design (TVD), and Lean Project Scheduling (PS).

Chapter 6, *Starting the Lean Construction Journey*, guides the reader through a proven implementation strategy. This strategy includes a review of the organization's change prerequisites, the question of organization assessments, the need for a Lean Facilitator, the use of consultants, and the issues of the Lean Construction Supply Chain.

This chapter also reviews the requirement of training all the organization's associates in Lean principles—a step often left out by many organizations that know the cost of the training but do not know or understand the cost of not doing this training. This mistake is painfully discovered later when the implementation falters.

And Finally ...

Instead of references to the sometimes confusing term "top management" of an organization, this book talks about an organization's Leadership Team. A typical Leadership Team includes the CEO, President, General Manager, or Project Manager (the top ranking manager in a facility) and their staffs.

This book was visioned to be a short, quick read. Its goal is to be an introduction and overview of Lean Construction so construction organizations can start a Lean implementation headed in the right direction.

This book is designed to be used as an internal training text. However, while the definition and use of the Lean Tools in construction is discussed in this book, their actual use in organizations (depending on the organization's Lean background and experience) may require further education. The references given at the end of each chapter can be a starting point.

References

Angelo, Ted. "Lean Overview" (Powerpoint Presentation). Grunau Company, Milwaukee, WI.

Bryson, B. and Yetmen, C. (2010) *The Owner's Dilemma: Driving Success and Innovation in the Design and Construction Industry*. Atlanta, GA: Östberg Library of Design Management, Greenway Communications.

Covey, S. (1996) *The Seven Habits of Highly Effective People*. Provo, UT: Franklin Covey.

Howell, G. "Origins of Lean Construction". Lean Construction Institute, http://leanconstruction.org.

"Integrated Project Delivery" is the Trademark of Westbrook Commercial Services.

"Last Planner" is the Registered Trademark of the Lean Construction Institute, http://leanconstruction.org.

LePatner, B. (2007) *Broken Buildings, Busted Budgets: How to Fix America's Trillion-Dollar Construction Industry*. Chicago: University of Chicago.

U.S. Department of Commerce, Bureau of Labor Statistics.

Chapter 1

An Introduction to Lean

Historically, Lean comes from the Toyota Production System (TPS), which has its roots in American manufacturing going all the way back to Henry Ford. Even today, Henry Ford is still a hero to the Japanese. Up until 1990, this system was called either TPS or World Class Manufacturing. In 1990, some Americans, studying the Toyota system, coined the term "Lean Production"—and it stuck.

TPS was created after WWII, when Toyota, lacking the finances to compete with American car manufacturing as they saw it during their visits in the 1950s, had to figure out how to do more with less. This need led to the identification of what was "customer value added" and what was "waste." The Lean Tools, including Setup Reduction, Standard Work, 5S, and Kanbans, were then developed to allow Toyota to do more with less by eliminating wasteful activities.

TPS has two main pillars:

- Respect for people
- Continuous improvement (Kaizen)

Respect for people involves creating a culture in which people are recognized as the organization's most valuable resource and then are trained and motivated to use their ideas to eliminate waste and improve processes on a continuous basis.

Kaizen is a Japanese word that means to "change for the good"—doing little things better every day—continuous improvement (CI). Kaizen is an integral part of the Toyota culture. This philosophy is why the Japanese are such good problem solvers—they view all problems as opportunities to improve.

Thus, Lean, at its core, is about eliminating waste in our businesses to maximize the value we add to the project and ultimately provide owner/customer satisfaction. To be considered a value adding activity, the activity must meet all three of the following requirements:

- It must change the shape or form of the item. For example, creating an architectural model or hanging drywall.
- The owner must care about the activity and be willing to pay for it.
- The activity must be completed correctly the first time. Owners are unwilling to pay for rework or repair.

A company's view of what is value added and what is waste is distorted by its experience of doing wasteful things for the past 20 or so years. "We've always done it this way, so we must need to do it. How can it be waste?"

A good example of how our view of what is value added is distorted comes from the administrative area—invoices from suppliers. What happens if we put this process under the light of "Is it value added or waste?" The purchasing process basically looks like this:

1. An order for an item is placed with the supplier. In general, we know what the price of the item is at this point.

2. The item ships, we receive the item, and someone signs off that...we ordered 10 and received 10.

At this point, we know what the price is and the amount of the item received. (Either shipping charges are added to the packing list, or items ship FOB your facility.) We could now pay the supplier. But instead, we force the supplier to create an Accounts Receivable (A/R) department to create and send an invoice to tell us what we already know. The next question is, "Who pays for the cost of the supplier's A/R department?" The customer!

Another way to think about the question "Is this value added or waste?" is to look at it this way. If the activity was added as a single line item to the customer's invoice (and not hidden in a lump sum amount), would the customer be willing to pay for it? For example:

Hours	**Activity**	**Price**
25 hours	Made 100 trips back to the gangbox to complete the electrical	$1,250.00

Obviously, the answer is no! Why would any owner want to pay for our wasteful work practices?

The nemesis of value adding is waste (or non-value added time). *Waste* is defined as anything the owner is unwilling to pay for. Waste adds cost but provides no value to the owner. An example of waste in the office might be the waste of time searching and hunting for hard copy files, office supplies, drawings, computer files, and so on. On the jobsite, waste is anything that prevents "tool time"—the actual creating and building of the project the trades were hired to do. Examples of jobsite waste (reductions in tool time) are miscommunication in the office causing jobsite delays when RFIs are required or the unnecessary multiple handling and moving of materials before installation.

The trouble with waste is that it makes us less competitive. Waste is part of our current processes, so it is difficult to identify because we have always done it. This wasted time and these wasted activities must be paid for in the wages and salaries of our people (and sometimes in material). These non-value added activities are then included in our bid prices, making these bids less competitive.

Organizational waste in the administrative area and at the jobsite comes in eight categories:

1. Scrap/Rework/Defects/Reconciliations

- Misunderstanding requirements
- Fabrication defects
- Incomplete or wrong info/data/material
- Incorrect installation

2. Transportation—Material or Information Handling

- Jobsite material movement
- Uncoordinated trucking deliveries
- Lack of identification and resorting
- Poor site layout resulting in long transportation distances

3. Motion

- Hunting and searching for tools, equipment, office supplies, information on a computer, drawings—anything!
- Not completing work while in one area
- Going to pick up forgotten material
- Poor jobsite organization

4. **Waiting/Delays**
    - Waiting for RFIs, tools, instructions, materials, a supplier—anything!
    - Waiting for other work to be completed

5. **Inventory**
    - Not pre-planning what parts are needed
    - Fabricating job too early
    - Over-purchasing "just in case"
    - Not returning excess material to vendors

6. **Overproduction**
    - Working out of sequence to try to get ahead
    - Creating extras of anything (i.e., paper copies) that end up in the trash
    - Anything at the jobsite that ends up in the dumpster (estimated at typically 9% by weight)

7. **Overprocessing**
    - Doing anything the owner/customer would not recognize as value
    - Selling Chevy, installing Cadillac

8. **Underutilized Human Resources**
    - Not using the brains and talents of the entire organization
    - Not recognizing that the "team decision" will be the best decision!

Based on our experience, for American businesses, Underutilized Human Resources (category 8) is the greatest form of waste. Note that in Taiichi Ohno's original definition of business waste at Toyota, there were seven categories (1-7 above). Number eight was added by Americans for American organizations because we have difficulty forming teams and have never fully used our human resources. We lack the homogenous population that shortens the team-building process time and a "respect for people" culture that is prevalent in Japanese society, versus our value of "rugged individualism." One only needs to read about how the Japanese people acted after their 2011 tsunami to recognize this admirable difference. (For example, there was no looting, and millions of dollars in lost money was returned to its rightful owners.)

As was noted earlier, Lean's goal is to drive out waste to increase the value supplied to the owner, thereby improving owner satisfaction. This is a difficult concept for American companies because of our belief, through experience, that raising the level of owner satisfaction will cost more money. This perception is shown in the figure below.

Figure 1.1
The Perceived Cost of Owner Satisfaction

With Lean, the roadblock to owner satisfaction—waste—is eliminated, and owner satisfaction is automatically improved as costs, quality, and lead times are improved. When Lean is applied to the project and waste is eliminated, the cost of owner satisfaction actually goes down, not up, as shown in the following figure.

Figure 1.2
The Actual Cost of Owner Satisfaction with Lean

It is important to understand that success with Lean is not about working harder; it is about working smarter. Figures 1.3 and 1.4 illustrate this point. They represent an organization video recording a person from an administrative area and a person from a jobsite area for an entire day/shift. The day following the video recording, we sat down with these associates and reviewed the video, segregated their activities for the day, and created Figure 1.3.

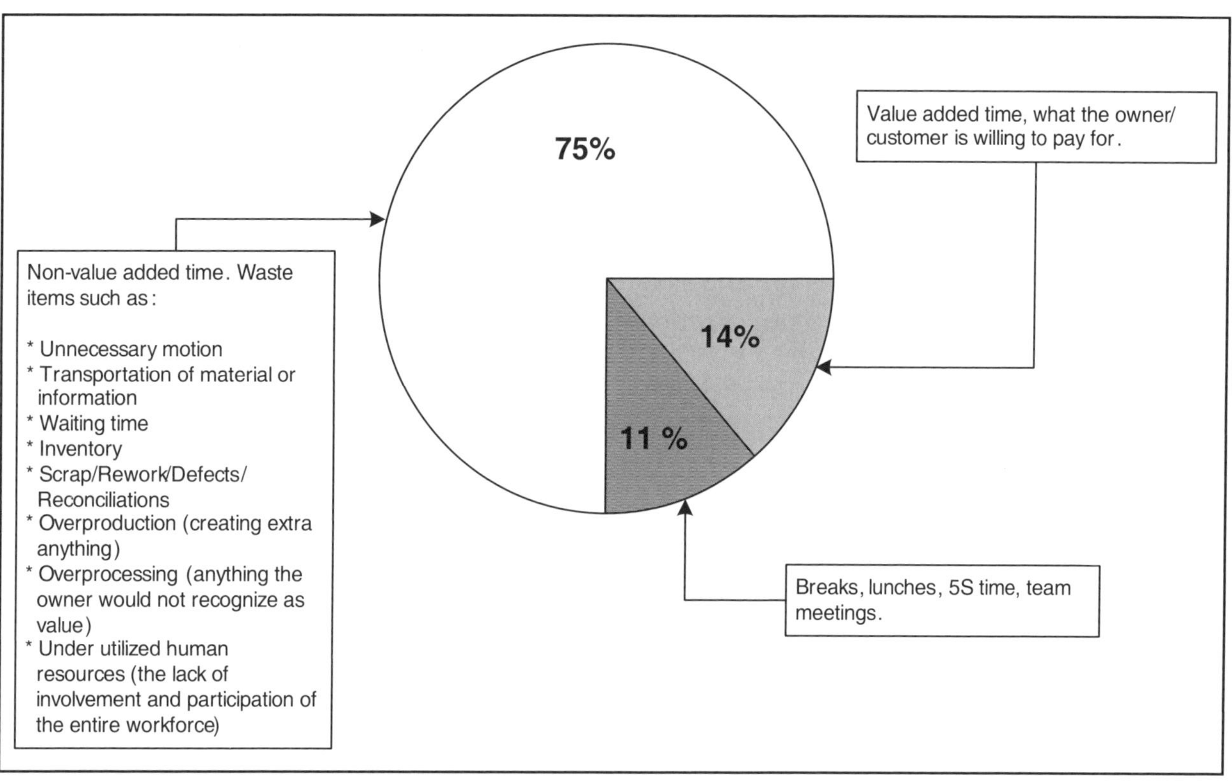

Figure 1.3
Typical Organization Productivity

In Figure 1.3, we see that 11% of the day was spent on breaks, lunches, 5S time, and team meetings. 5S is a Lean tool that helps create work areas that are safe, clean, organized, and ergonomically correct. 5S eliminates searching, looking, or hunting for anything. As business managers, we are happy with this 11%. We want our people doing these things.

The next part of the pie chart, 14%, was the part of the day spent doing things the owners would pay us to do (adding value). If we showed this part of the video to the owners, they would say, "Yes, we are willing to pay that person to do that step."

The remainder of the pie chart, 75%, was spent on items the owner would not be willing to pay for (if we asked them) because they do not add value, but add cost. It is not that people are not working—they are. The problem is they are doing activities the owner will not pay them to do, and if the owner is not paying them, the company is, and it is either coming right out of profits or making our proposals less competitive.

Productivity improvements occur when we stop doing wasteful activities and substitute value-adding activities.

This is the point where we believe companies get confused about their ability to compete. Companies have pie charts that look like Figure 1.3, and their response is to chase low wages!

For the purpose of analyzing our ability to compete using Lean, let's assume a company has a composite pie chart (administrative, shops, and the jobsite) that looks like Figure 1.3 and is paying its people an average of $40.00 per hour. If, over a period of time, the company were able to stop doing some wasteful activities and substitute value-adding activities, the pie chart could look like Figure 1.4:

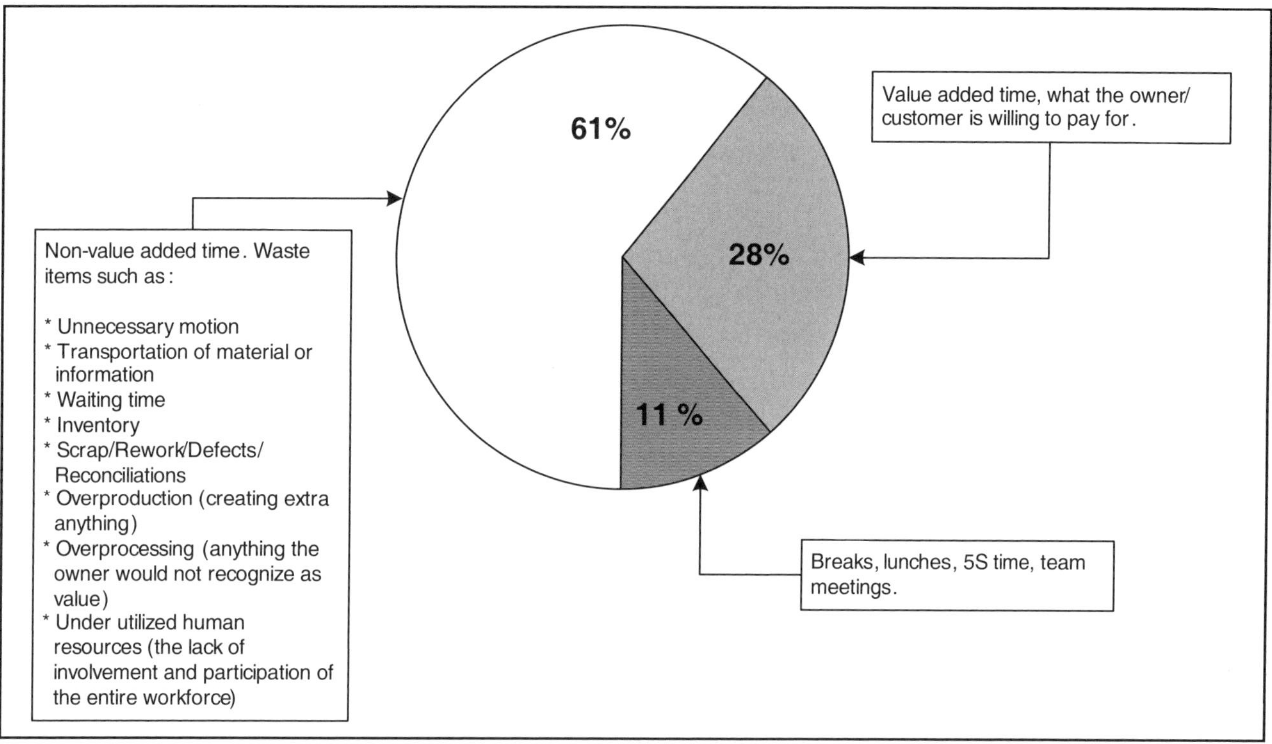

Figure 1.4
Productivity Improvements Available with Lean

What the company has effectively done (besides doubling its productivity) is to reduce its effective wage rate, as it appears to the competition, to $20.00 per hour. (Note that this chart shows another doubling in productivity is available.)

This pie chart shows the impact (and opportunity) of waste reduction and the corresponding increase that value added time has on productivity and, ultimately, the hours bid on a project.

Eliminating all of the white part of the pie can be difficult because some operations in the organization are non-value added—but necessary. For example, payroll: The owner does not care about payroll, but if you stop paying your people, you are out of business. Therefore, the non-value added but necessary operations in the white part of the pie, such as payroll, need to be accomplished as accurately and quickly as possible.

Once organizational waste is identified, the purpose of the Lean Tools (such as 5S) is to eliminate that waste. It is important to note again that the waste identified for elimination with the Lean Tools is waste recognized during Lean Policy Deployment (Chapter 2) as barriers to achieving the business goals. All companies starting the Lean journey have hundreds of areas that could be improved with Lean; Policy Deployment ensures that we will start improving the areas that provide the desired business results.

As noted in the introduction, because the amount of waste varies widely by industry, Lean is often classified into four industry categories: Lean Manufacturing, Lean Construction, Lean Healthcare, and Lean Service. For Lean Construction, the Lean Tools are divided into two groups: the Core Lean Tools, which apply to all industries, and the Lean Construction Tools, which include the tools that are project based. These groups are shown in the following figure.

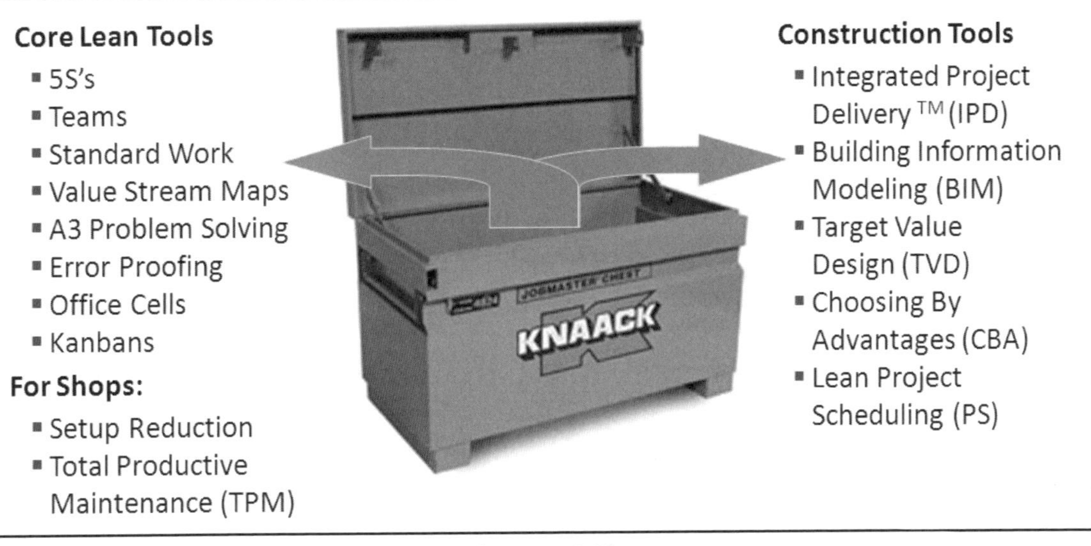

Figure 1.5
Lean Construction Tools

The definition and use of the Core Lean Tools are included in Chapter 4. The definition and use of the Lean Construction Tools are included in Chapter 5.

Core Lean Tools and the Lean Construction Tools—Is There A Difference?

Note that some of the Lean Construction Tools have analogs in manufacturing. Target Value Design is Value Engineering/Value Analysis, and a small part of BIM's construction project capability is Manufacturing Design Engineering software programs that can load designs directly into the machine tools that will create the part. Choosing By Advantages (CBA) has no analog in any other industry. However, because it is an extremely powerful decisionmaking tool, it ultimately will become part of the Core Lean Toolbox.

Integrated Project Delivery (IPD) and Lean Project Scheduling (PS) are tools that represent particular challenges to Lean Construction. These challenges are not to the mechanics of the tools but to the development of the support structure required to consider the use of the tool for the project. IPD, which can create win-win solutions for the project team, requires the owner's commitment.

Both tools require great two-way communication, trust, and teamwork in an environment where projects are collective, collaborative, and (currently) competitive activities. These requirements add a level of challenge to teamwork not found in other industries. Currently, a new project means new trade partners, new suppliers, and new teams who may have no previous experience with Lean Construction and who may have been a competitor on a previous project. This change requires time for team and relationship building all over again.

It has been said that the teamwork required to support IPD and PS can be learned on the job—a position we would strongly disagree with. We are not born leaders or teammates, and therefore, construction associates should be trained in what a good team and team members look like, as well as the symptoms of a dysfunctional team.

At some time in the future, Lean Construction will pick trade partners and suppliers like Lean Manufacturing picks parts suppliers—by who can deliver their part (project) for the lowest total cost, not by the piece part price (bid). Total cost includes quality, delivery to schedule, lead time, adoption of Lean as a continuous improvement process (to hold or reduce costs), and price. We will discuss these elements further in Chapters 2 and 6.

Lean Construction is Lean with the addition of a few tools that are particular to construction. The keys to Lean success required in other Lean industry categories—Lean Planning and Lean Culture—are also required in Lean Construction. We will further discuss the keys to success with Lean, regardless of the industry, in Chapters 2 and 3.

References

Angelo, Ted. "Lean Overview" (Powerpoint Presentation). Grunau Company, Milwaukee, WI.

Donaldson, James, S. & Goldman, R. (2011, March 15) Japanese, waiting in line for hours, follow social order after quake. *ABC News*. Retrieved from http://abcnews.go.com/Health/japan-victims-show-resilience-earthquake-tsunami-sign-sense/story?id=13135355

Fayad, V. and Rubrich, L. (2009) *Policy Deployment and Lean Implementation Planning* (Rev. ed.). Fort Wayne, IN: WCM Associates LLC.

Rubrich, L. & Watson, M. (2004) *Implementing World Class Manufacturing* (2nd ed.). Fort Wayne, IN: WCM Associates LLC.

Solomon, J. (2007) *Accounting for World Class Operations.* Fort Wayne, IN: WCM Associates LLC.

The Lean Construction Institute, http://leanconstruction.org)

Chapter 2

Planning the Lean Construction Implementation

"Begin with the End in Mind"

- Steven Covey

7 Habits of Highly Effective People

10 Steps to Successful Policy Deployment

1. Establish a Mission and Behavioral Expectations
2. Develop Business Goals
3. Brainstorm for Opportunities to Achieve Goals
4. Define Parameters to Value Opportunities
5. Establish Weighting Requirements, Rate Opportunities, and Prioritize
6. Conduct a Reality Check
7. Develop Lean Implementation Plan
8. Develop Bowling Chart
9. Develop Countermeasures
10. Conduct Business Reviews

This chapter covers the development of the four components of Lean and how they fit into the 10 Step Lean Policy Deployment process (shown in the left column) for deploying Lean as the operating system in an organization so the desired business results can be achieved.

American organizations have difficulty sustaining Lean improvements to achieve any real business results. While often there is a spurt in activities and improvements early in the Lean implementation, these changes slow down and stall when the organization begins to realize:

- Lean is not a "magic pill" or "silver bullet" for the organization's problems.
- A Lean implementation requires difficult and company-wide change, especially for top management.
- Not everyone thinks that Lean applies to them (i.e., estimating, IT, project management, human resources, and other key areas).
- Quick bottom-line results do not appear, giving rise to questions about a payback from the investment in Lean.
- Top management support for the change necessary to implement Lean is limited or missing.

To be successful with Lean, we must view and acknowledge Lean as the "operating system" by which we will run the entire organization and achieve the desired results. Lean is not just a set of Lean tools used at the jobsite—for example, 5S or Lean Project Scheduling (Last Planner®). Achieving the "desired results" means being focused on the three key metrics by which all "for profit" companies are measured: profit, cash flow, and revenue growth. Chapter 1 noted how the linkage between desired results and Lean is accomplished using a technique called Policy Deployment. The Lean tools are deployed only when we understand how their use will help eliminate the wasteful activities that are preventing us from achieving the desired results.

Getting U.S. organizations to grasp the idea of adopting Lean as an operating system in their attempts to implement Lean has been very difficult to accomplish because it is rarely understood as an absolute requirement to a successful implementation. This problem has resulted in an extremely low level of Lean success as measured by either the ability to achieve "World Class" (globally competitive) status or achieve significant results from an organization's Lean activities.

The September 30th 2011 edition of *Manufacturing and Technology News* magazine presented an article entitled "Lean and Six Sigma Are Not Leading To Breakthroughs In Corporate Performance." This article, the result of a survey of 100 business executives conducted by AlixPartners, a business consulting firm, highlighted some problems with Lean and Six Sigma implementations including the following:

- 70% of reporting organizations reported a less than 5% improvement in manufacturing costs as a result of Lean.
- 60% of respondents said their previous Lean improvements were not sustainable.
- Only 17% of respondents reported seeking long-term culture change in their organization.

AlixPartners made observations about the survey, summarized below:

- Most companies are seeing a poor return on their investment in Lean and Six Sigma.
- Companies are far too focused on implementing Lean tools and processes rather than on basic execution.
- Organizations need to dramatically rethink their Lean strategies—focusing on cash and finding the biggest opportunity to improve and then deciding which Lean tool(s) will help them achieve that result.
- Company Leadership Teams must take responsibility for the Lean implementation rather than trying to push this responsibility down to the Lean facilitator.

This article supported information that was previously reported by *Industry Week* magazine. As shown in the following figure, 74% of American businesses that indicated they were using Lean as their business improvement activity reported "little progress" or "no progress" to *Industry Week* concerning their Lean implementations. Toyota purportedly says they believe 70% of American companies are making little progress with Lean.

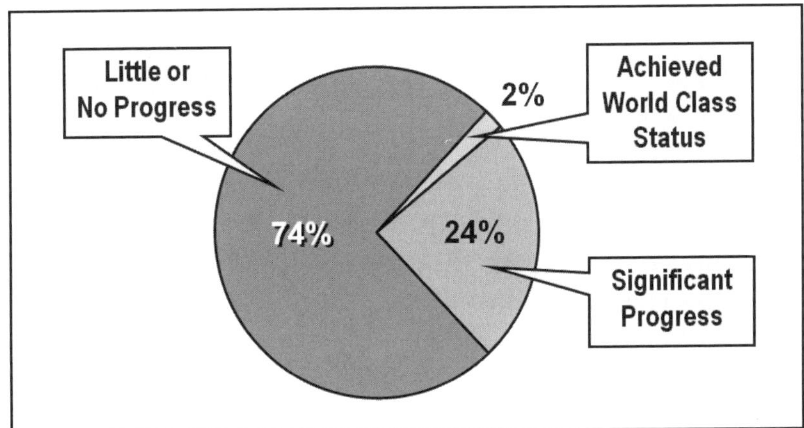

Figure 2.1
American Lean Business Results
(Reference: *Industry Week*, 2007)

For the "little or no progress" organizations, Lean is viewed as an appendage or an add-on, something that is done in addition to their normal busy schedules, not as the operating system by which they run the organization and achieve their business goals. This lack of progress leaves organizations saying: "We're different. Lean doesn't work for us." Thus, they place the lack of results on Lean itself rather than on the organization's Lean implementation plan.

Lean as a System

World Class business results cannot be achieved without the "Lean thinking" that comes from deploying Lean as a system throughout the organization. Lean thinking is the elimination of waste to achieve an organization's goals—and it must saturate companywide discussions and activities. If Lean is viewed as the operating system, with people at the center of Continuous Improvement (CI) activities, then the Human Resources area and the company culture must be viewed as important components in the development of this operating system. Creating a Lean Culture is further discussed in Chapter 3.

Lean begins with the implementation of the four components of Lean and ends with the organization successfully achieving its business goals through the use of Policy Deployment.

Why Lean?

Before beginning the four components of the Lean implementation process, an organization's Leadership Team starts by asking themselves, "Why do we want to do Lean?" The expected answer is "To create an organization that works safely and makes money." (Even not-for-profit organizations want this.)

The Japanese have an interesting way of describing the impact of Lean on owners/customers. They say, "Profits are the reward of a satisfied customer." Everyone can relate to this saying because it is how most people operate with/shop for/choose suppliers in their personal lives. This saying is depicted in the following figure.

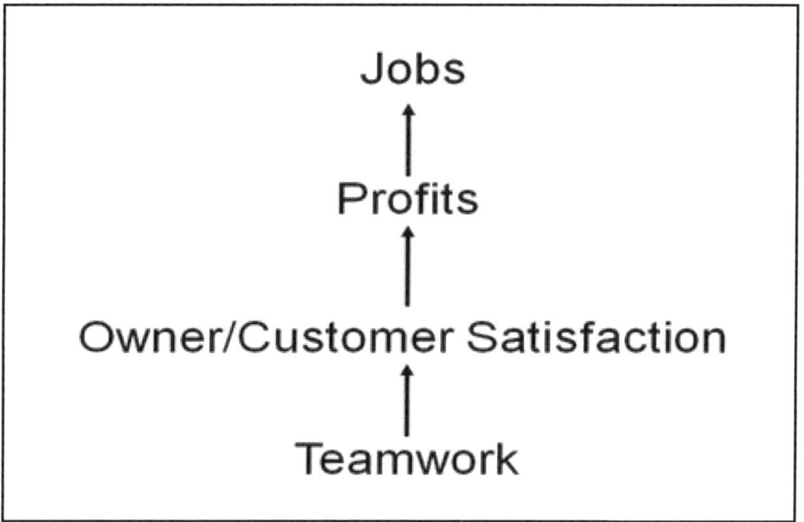

Figure 2.2
Profits are the Reward of Owner/Customer Satisfaction

This figure also dispels the rumor that Lean is about "cutting heads." Clearly, it is about growing a profitable business by taking business away from less able competitors, domestic or foreign.

The figure also shows the requirement for organizational and project-wide teamwork to achieve owner satisfaction. Frankly, this is a difficult challenge in construction because of the variety of organizations that are involved in a project. In addition, the current practice is that this entire group may never work on the same project together again. Unfortunately, this requirement for teamwork is currently not being directly addressed by construction organizations. The current thinking is that teamwork will develop in organizations as they are exposed to more and more Lean projects. This approach is extremely slow and precariously uneven. No organizational culture change occurs, and project improvements are not institutionalized. Projects should start with at least a foundation of Lean teamwork principles given to all team members.

In Lean Manufacturing, the idea of a Lean Supply Chain is prevalent. Often, it is thought that the most valuable member of the supply chain is the truck driver who does not drop the product off the end of a truck before delivering it to the customer. Lean Manufacturing generally measures suppliers in five different areas:

- Quality
- On-time delivery
- Lead time
- Continuous Improvement activities (Lean and Six Sigma) that support reducing or holding costs
- Price

Suppliers are selected according to who has the lowest "total acquisition cost" of these five measures. Often, the selected supplier does not have the lowest piece price. Ideally, in the future, CMs and GCs will use preferred Lean suppliers and trade partners that are measured on "total project cost" as opposed to just the bid price.

The impetus for a Lean Construction Supply Chain must come from as close to the owner in the process as possible. This motivation can be achieved in a Design-Build or IPD environment if the CM or GC recognizes that, if they want a World Class project, they must have World Class suppliers and trade partners or when they begin to understand that the project will be no better than their worst supplier or trade partner. Lean Construction Supply Chain will be discussed further in Chapter 6.

Lean Planning—Beginning with the End in Mind—Required Business Results

Now that we understand why a Lean implementation is necessary, the first component—Lean Planning—can be discussed.

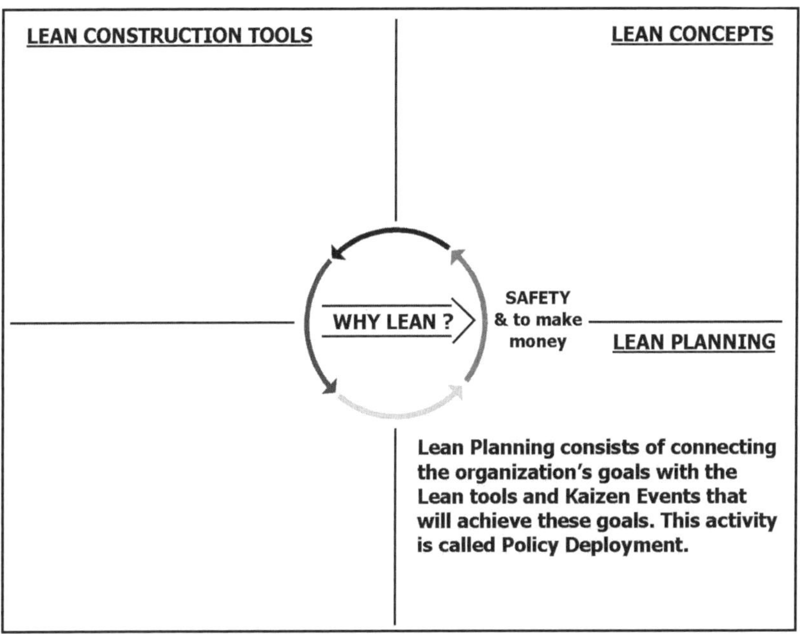

Figure 2.3
Four Components of Lean—Lean Planning

The commitment to Lean Planning as the first component of Lean ensures Lean will not be used as an add-on or appendage in the organization, but as a system to accomplish the #1 objective—the organization's goals. To do otherwise reduces an organization's opportunity to fully use the power of Lean through the complete participation and involvement of the entire workforce.

Lean creates value for your owner/customer. As a for-profit organization, the reward for creating owner value is measured in terms of the organization's ability to make money, normally measured as Operating Income, Earnings Before Interest, Taxes, Depreciation, and Amortization (EBITDA), or Net Income. Some organizations say that measuring Return on Invested Capital (ROIC) and Economic Value Added (EVA) are better measures of creating value. Regardless of how profit is measured or reported, the significance is the same: if you are not making money, you will go out of business or you will be getting a lot of "adult help" from some corporate office.

Cash Flow is also very important. If you do not have money to make payroll, you must either borrow money or go out of business. Borrowing money is expensive and creates no value for your organization. Going out of business should not be an option.

Revenue growth should be considered only once the organization is profitable and has good cash flow. Why would any organization have a growth strategy if it is not currently profitable? Many companies think they would be more profitable if they had more business. Once again, wrong! Size the organization and make it profitable; then consistently grow the business profitably.

One of the first activities in Lean Planning is the Leadership Team establishing high-level goals for the organization. This is Step 2 in the Policy Deployment process after establishing a mission and guiding principles/behavioral expectations. These goals should focus on the business vision and strategic objectives and should be stated in the SMART goal format shown in the following examples:

- We will achieve 0 lost-day injuries for the next 12 months.

- We will improve our operating income from 8% to 12% in the next 12 months.
- We will increase the number of owners we provide building services for from 80 to 120 with the same resources within the next 18 months.
- We will improve our inventory turns from 6 to 10 over the next 12 months.
- We will grow our business through new projects and services from $40M to $50M over the next 24 months.

SMART goals are:

Specific
Measurable
Achievable
Relevant
Time Dimensioned

Note that, for most organizations, the high-level business goals are financial in nature. Most of the organization's associates do not know or understand exactly how their jobs affect the financials. Policy Deployment converts these financial goals into operational improvements that can achieve those financial goals. Operation associates are asked only for ideas on how to eliminate the wasteful activities in their jobs.

The Leadership Team must limit the number of goals. It is recommended that three to five goals are established. If the number of goals exceeds five, people do not remember them and no longer use them to guide their decisionmaking processes. Remember: three to five goals only!

One of the goals must always be SAFETY. The only thing that takes precedence over business objectives is safety. The goal for safety must always be zero incidents. Note that, for the many companies that are already reporting "lost injury" (lost time) days, their initial goal should be zero lost injury days. All identifiable safety issues must be dealt with immediately. World Class organizations have a clear policy statement that effectively communicates that the company will "provide a safe, clean, neat, and organized working environment" for all associates. (These are the goals of the 5S tool also.)

Lean Concepts

The component of Lean Concepts, like Lean itself, is simple: it is the elimination of waste to improve the flow of information and material throughout the entire organization and jobsite (the system). Lean Concepts define the eight types of construction waste as discussed in Chapter 1 and shown in the left column.

8 Types of Construction Waste

1. Scrap/Rework/Defects/ Reconciliations
2. Transportation—Material or Information Handling
3. Motion
4. Waiting/Delays
5. Inventory
6. Overproduction
7. Overprocessing
8. Underutilized Human Resources

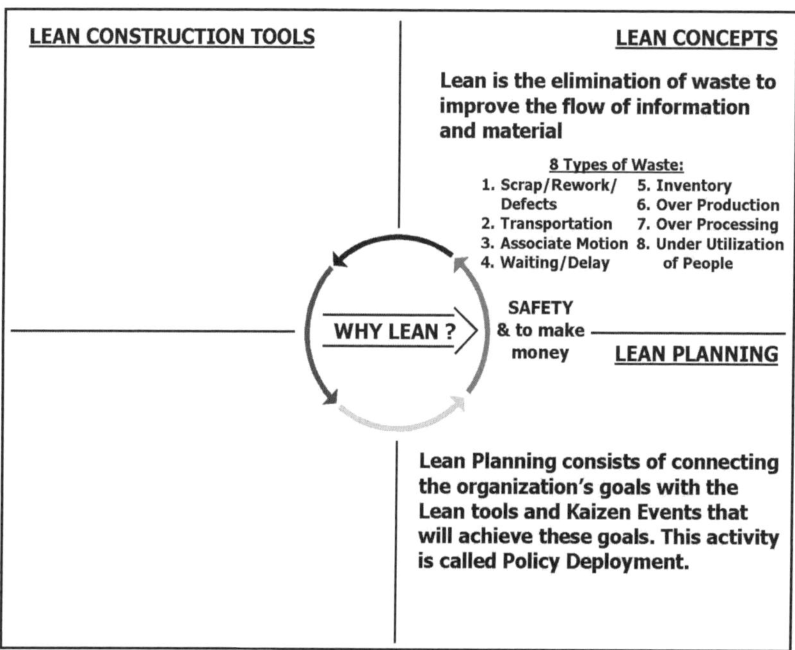

Figure 2.4
Four Components of Lean—Lean Concepts

Waste is created when the flow of the project stops.

Remember, for an activity to be value added (not waste), it must meet all three of the following criteria:

- It must change the shape or form of the item. For example, turning sheet metal into HVAC ducting or installing plumbing fixtures.
- The owner must care about the activity and be willing to pay for it.
- The activity must be completed correctly the first time. Owners are unwilling to pay for rework or repair.

Lean Construction Tools

After developing organizational goals using the Lean Planning component and understanding how wasteful activities in our organizations prevent the achievement of those goals (Lean Concepts), the discussion can now turn to understanding the Lean Construction tools. These tools, as shown in Figure 2.5 below, serve two purposes. They identify the waste preventing the organization from reaching its goals and provide a tool for eliminating or reducing the identified waste.

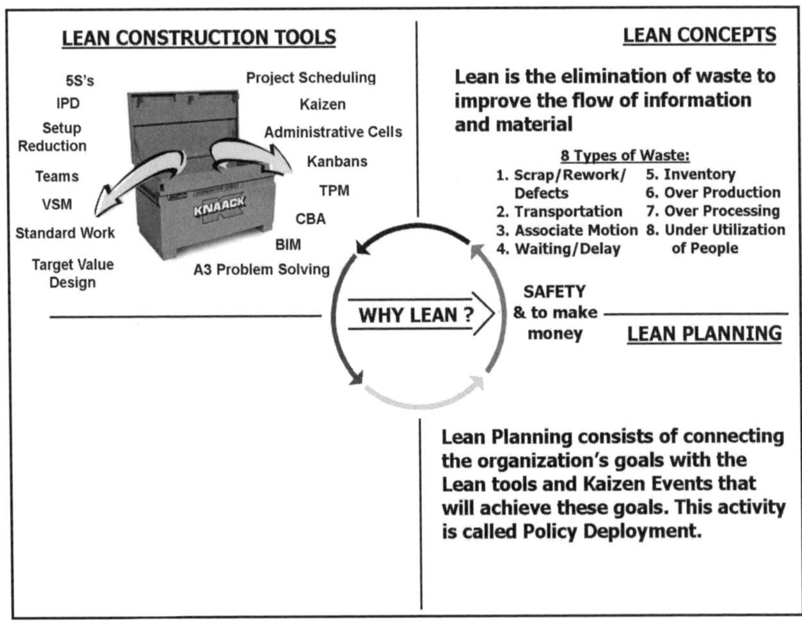

Figure 2.5
Four Components of Lean—
Lean Construction Tools

For example, the Value Stream Mapping (VSM) tool's sole purpose is to identify waste. The remaining tools are then used to eliminate/reduce the waste that was identified in the VSM. If we identified in Lean Concepts that a particular project process was slow and had a long lead time, a VSM would be created to identify where the stoppages, waiting, and delays are occurring. If those delays are related to material or supply outages and shortages, the solution might be to implement the inventory replenishment tool—kanbans—or a variation of this tool—supplier managed inventories. If the delays are related to searching, hunting, and looking for items, files, drawings, or materials, the solution would be to implement the 5S tool. The goal of 5S is to create a safe, clean, and organized working environment, thus eliminating the need to search for anything. Detailed discussion of the Lean Construction Tools occurs in Chapters 4 and 5.

Without the connection between the use of the Lean Tools and the business objectives of the organization, people do not understand WHY they are doing what they are doing.

As noted earlier, the Lean Construction Tools area is where most organizations become confused and go off track with their Lean implementation. They think that, by implementing some of the tools, they will have a Lean organization. Skipping Lean Planning and Lean Culture prevents the improvements made by only using the tools from being sustainable, as mentioned in the *Manufacturing and Technology News* article.

Lean Culture

The fourth component for implementing Lean is establishing a Lean Culture (Figure 2.6). Lean, as an organizational system, can only be built on the foundation of a Lean Culture.

Lean Culture is the component that makes it all happen, the component that musters the organization's most important resource—its people—to create an organizational "war on wasteful activities."

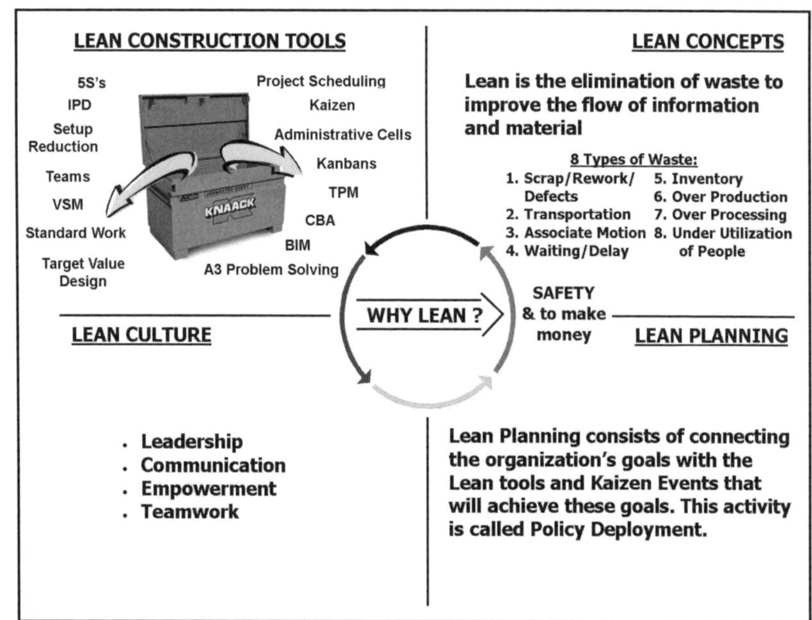

Figure 2.6
Four Components of Lean—Lean Culture

The only major competitive weapon an organization has is its people. Most organizations do not have a lot of patents or technology that can protect them from their competitors or create barriers to entry into their markets. Generally speaking, it is the organization's people who make the difference.

What is culture? William A. Haviland in his textbook *Cultural Anthropology* defines it as follows:

> A set of rules and standards shared by members of a society, which when acted upon the members, produce behavior that falls within a range the members consider proper and acceptable.

Culture is a learned set of beliefs and behaviors and is developed by the organization as a response to the working environment established by the organization's leadership and management team.

A culture is established in all organizations, regardless of whether its development is guided or unguided.

Developing Lean Culture begins with the development of the guiding principles or behavioral expectations during Lean Planning. Because the principles and expectations are developed in Lean Planning by the organization's Leadership Team, these expectations set the framework to be filled in by the following Lean Culture elements:

- Leadership
- Communication
- Empowerment
- Teamwork

Every organization has a culture, whether the Leadership Team has guided its development or the culture has developed on its own. Culture can have a positive or negative effect on an organization's performance. Chapter 3 is devoted to the development of a Lean Culture.

To be successful with Lean, a company must be in balance. It must achieve the correct balance in using Lean Planning, understanding Lean Concepts, using the correct Lean Tools, and empowering its workforce by creating a Lean Culture. However, you must have all four components in process before you can announce that you are truly on the Lean Construction journey.

Culture is a learned set of beliefs and behaviors. We begin to learn our culture from our mother and father, aunts and uncles, brothers and sisters, and our extended family. We learn what is right and what is wrong. We learn what behavior is acceptable and what behavior is unacceptable.

Putting the System Together—Policy Deployment and Lean Implementation Planning

As noted in the Introduction, this section is required reading for the Leadership Team. Others may just skim or skip the PD section.

Policy Deployment (Toyota calls its version Hoshin Kanri) is a process by which organizations deploy specific Lean activities/Kaizen Events throughout the organization so that the company's annual goals and strategic out-year goals can be achieved. In these organizations, to prevent the dilution or overloading of their human resources, no other Lean activities occur other than those specified in Policy Deployment.

The purpose of this section is to provide an overview of the Policy Deployment (PD) process so readers can understand the power and the basic steps of the PD process. This understanding will help them to understand their role in a successful PD activity. For the Lean Facilitator who must guide the Leadership Team through this process, a complete PD creation guidebook with spreadsheet templates is listed in the references at the end of this chapter.

The PD process, which meshes with the four components of Lean, has 10 steps. The PD process is completed annually following the same time-frame as budgeting and strategic planning processes for the upcoming year. In most organizations, PD covers basically the same material, with generally much more organizational input, feedback, and planning; therefore, it can replace both the budgeting and strategic planning processes. The PD process consists of the following 10 steps (see Figure 2.7). Because resource availability is always an issue, the first time this process is completed (because we are doing our normal fire fighting and now fire prevention simultaneously), we have included some resource guidelines to use for each step:

Step #	Step Definition	Resource Guidelines
1	Establish a Mission and Behavioral Expectations	Leadership Team
2	Develop Business Goals	Leadership Team
3	Brainstorm for Opportunities to Achieve Goals	Project Managers, Foremen, Superintendents, Supervisors, Middle Managers & Leadership Team
4	Define Parameters to Value Opportunities	Leadership Team
5	Establish Weighting Requirements, Rate Opportunities and Prioritize	Leadership Team
6	Conduct a Reality Check	Leadership Team
7	Develop Lean Implementation Plan	Project Managers, Foremen, Superintendents, Supervisors, Middle Managers & Leadership Team
8	Develop Bowling Chart	Project Managers, Foremen, Superintendents, Supervisors, Middle Managers & Leadership Team
9	Develop Countermeasures	Leadership Team
10	Conduct Business Monthly Reviews	Project Managers, Foremen, Superintendents, Supervisors, Middle Managers & Leadership Team

Figure 2.7
10-Step Policy Deployment Process
& Resource Guidelines

Understand that except for Steps 1 and 2, in which, generally, only the Leadership Team has the vision and knowledge of where the organization should be going and what it needs to achieve, these resources are minimums. Leaving the supervisors, managers, foremen, superintendents, and project managers out of any of the noted steps is fatal to this process. Their ideas, involvement, participation, buy-in, ownership, and accountability, as well as that of their associates, are vital to the success of this process.

10 Steps to Successful Policy Deployment

1. Establish a Mission and Behavioral Expectations
2. Develop Business Goals
3. Brainstorm for Opportunities to Achieve Goals
4. Define Parameters to Value Opportunities
5. Establish Weighting Requirements, Rate Opportunities, and Prioritize
6. Conduct a Reality Check
7. Develop Lean Implementation Plan
8. Develop Bowling Chart
9. Develop Countermeasures
10. Conduct Business Reviews

Step 1—Establish a Mission and Behavioral Expectations

Mission Statement

The single greatest characteristic of a good leader is the ability to create a vision for the future (the late Steve Jobs of Apple, for example). What will the company need to look like in one, three, and five years to still be competitive and growing?

In this book, the terms *Mission* and *Vision* are used almost interchangeably. While "semi-strict" definitions exist, most organizations are either confused about the difference or define the terms differently. It is important that organizations do not get hung-up on terminology. The important concept is that the Leadership Team creates a picture of where the organization must be at some point in the future, and then, as futurist Joel Barker said in his Leadershift video, "build bridges" to that future.

Step 1 requires the company to have a clear, concise Mission Statement that will provide focus and aid the organization in decisionmaking.

One of Steven Covey's *Seven Habits of Highly Effective People* is to "Begin with the end in mind."

> When we begin with the end in mind, we have a personal direction to guide our daily activities, without which we will accomplish little toward our own goals. Beginning with the end

> in mind is part of the process of personal leadership, taking control of our own lives.
>
> Organizational mission statements should be developed by everyone in the organization. If there is no involvement in the process, there will be no commitment to the statement. The reward system must compliment [*sic*] and strengthen the stated value systems.
>
> An organization may have an all-encompassing mission statement, and each location, or even each team, may have their own. However, they should all dovetail with each other.
>
> If the mission statements of your family and organization dovetail with your personal mission statement, and you use those statements to keep your end in mind, you will accomplish your goals more quickly and easily.

Developing and communicating a clear Mission Statement can drive the decisionmaking process within an organization. It provides a focus and a direction. People can more easily stay focused on what they are doing rather than going back to management for permission to do something. They know where the organization is going, so they can spend more time on getting things done, creating a bias for action.

Thus, the Leadership Team must be able to work with the people to establish a plan that will make the Mission Statement happen. This Mission Statement and plan must be communicated to the entire organization over and over again.

Behavioral Expectations

The Leadership Team can jump-start the culture change process by issuing organizational behavioral expectations or what are sometimes called codes of conduct. Behavioral expectations or codes of conduct are short statements displayed throughout the organization. They are also printed on a laminated pocket card that is handed out to every associate. These statements are "a set of rules or standards" that members of the organization use to guide their behavior and actions. Behavioral expectations define the cultural aspects of "how" people do their jobs. They add a new dimension to individual or team performance evaluations that typically only measure performance—"what" employees have done. This combined culture and performance associate evaluation activity is discussed in Chapter 3.

It is interesting to note that many construction organizations have "values" and other principle statements about their culture posted in their companies—more than any other industry we have seen. However, it appears few of these companies actually have integrated these statements into their "operating system," thus leaving the values as just words.

Making these behavioral expectations part of the system includes integrating them into the hiring process, job descriptions, the new associate orientation program, performance reviews, merit reviews and promotion considerations.

A construction industry exception to the "values as just words" was discovered at the Grunau Company, a Milwaukee based MEP subcontractor. When asked why a particular person was not hired for an open position at

Grunau, the answer given by Ted Angelo, Executive Vice President, was "He didn't fit our culture." An example of Grunau's values statement is shown in Figure 2.8.

GRUNAU COMPANY STATEMENT OF VALUES

We require complete honesty and integrity.

We believe that individuals who are given responsibility and treated with respect, will give their best.

We make commitments with care, and live up to them.

We believe work is an important part of life that should be rewarding and enjoyable.

We guard and conserve the company's resources with the same vigilance that we use to guard and conserve our own personal resources.

We encourage safe work practices in every endeavor.

We insist on giving our best.

We focus on positive results regardless of the circumstances.

We believe that a clear understanding of our mission, goals, and our expectations of each other, is critical to our success.

We strive to be friendly and courteous, as well as fair and compassionate.

We encourage and support each other in our personal and professional endeavors.

Figure 2.8
Statement of Values/Behavioral Expectation

The Wiremold Company, an often used example of a very successful Lean implementation in an American company, used a code of conduct statement to reset the Wiremold culture at the start of their "do or die" Lean journey.

CODE OF CONDUCT

- Respect Others
- Tell The Truth
- Be Fair
- Try New Ideas
- Ask Why
- Keep Your Promises
- Do Your Share

Figure 2.9
Wiremold Code of Conduct

To reinforce the code at Wiremold, the Leadership Team members would circulate among the workforce on a regular basis, asking team members to "tell me one part of the code." An additional example of behavioral expectations or guiding principles is shown on the following page.

BiehnCo

Mission Statement

To be the customer recognized leader in cutting solutions by providing high quality, competitively priced, short lead-time, and reliably delivered products through an exceptional workforce trained and empowered to use Lean Enterprise as the method to continuously improve and create shareholder value.

Guiding Principles

* We will use 5S to maintain a SAFE, clean, neat, and organized work environment.

* We will strive to adhere to all customer requirements and to all BiehnCo policies, procedures, and work instructions.

* We will do the right thing even if no one is watching.

* We expect everyone to wage a *"war on waste"* and actively participate, in a team environment, to continuously improve all work processes.

* It is everyone's responsibility to provide and seek out training and development opportunities.

* We seek out root causes and make decisions based on valid data.

* We will demonstrate & encourage effective and timely two-way communications throughout BiehnCo.

* We expect punctuality and preparedness to support our team environment.

* We will respect people and diversity in the workplace, and behave in a positive, professional and ethical manner.

* We are personally responsible for our work and will take pride and ownership in everything we do.

* We will never knowingly walk by a safety, quality, or process nonconformance without taking action.

* We will respect company property and institute a TPM program to make our equipment more reliable.

Oct 2010

Figure 2.10
Combination Mission Statement and Behavioral Expectations
(Courtesy of CB Mfg. and Sales Co.)

Figure 2.10 shows an excellent example of a laminated card combination Mission Statement and Guiding Principles/Behavioral Expectations given out to all associates of this organization. It should be noted that the behavioral expectations will only produce culture change if they are modeled by the Leadership Team. Often, Leadership Teams want to create daunting lists of behavioral expectations because they feel that this is an

10 Steps to Successful Policy Deployment

1. Establish a Mission and Behavioral Expectations
2. Develop Business Goals
3. Brainstorm for Opportunities to Achieve Goals
4. Define Parameters to Value Opportunities
5. Establish Weighting Requirements, Rate Opportunities, and Prioritize
6. Conduct a Reality Check
7. Develop Lean Implementation Plan
8. Develop Bowling Chart
9. Develop Countermeasures
10. Conduct Business Reviews

opportunity to change the workforce culture. Unfortunately, in most organizations, it is the Leadership Team that requires the greatest degree of culture change. These daunting lists can really put the Leadership Team in the spotlight because everything the Leadership Team says or does (or doesn't do) sends a message.

Because the culture change process can take years, the Leadership Team must be committed to the behavioral expectations as a new way of doing business.

Step 2—Develop Business Goals

The guidelines for Step 2 were developed and completed in the discussion of the Lean Planning component starting on page 45.

As a result of that discussion, we will use the following SMART business goals for the purpose of explaining the rest of the PD Steps:

1. Achieve 0 lost day injuries for the next 12 months.
2. Improve Net Income from 3% to 8% of sales by the end of the fiscal year.
3. Improve Free Cash Flow from 30% to 70% of Net Income by the end of the fiscal year.
4. Increase Revenues from $32 million to $36 million without eroding margins by the end of the fiscal year.

Step 3—Brainstorm for Opportunities to Achieve These Goals

The purpose of this step is to use the knowledge, experience, and ideas of the organization's workforce to brainstorm opportunities to achieve the SMART business goals. There is a saying in brainstorming: if you want a lot of good ideas, have a lot of ideas. To generate a lot of ideas, the brainstorming group(s) must go as deep into the organization as possible. (We acknowledge doing so can be a difficult task.)

Additionally, this step begins the development of the workforce's "buy-in" to the Lean implementation process for these ideas. Ultimately, a group of these brainstormed ideas will be implemented by teams of people from the organization. If these teams or at least members of each team participated in the brainstorming activity, the implementations will go more quickly and be more successful.

To fully benefit from the people assigned to brainstorm for opportunities to achieve the goals developed in Step 2, this brainstorming team, which includes the Leadership Team, should have participated in a *Lean Construction Overview* training session (see page 248). The team must understand where all the waste elimination opportunities lie. Lean can solve any business problem, but before a plan can be developed to eliminate waste in your organization and solve the problem, you have to learn to "see" the waste.

Brainstorming is a critical step in the Policy Deployment process. A trained facilitator is required for this process to ensure that the team truly understands the rules for effective brainstorming so they can really identify all opportunities to achieve the goals. We know that

Step Staffing Guidelines:

Steps 1 & 2 - Leadership Team

Step 3 - Project Managers, Foremen, Superintendents, Supervisors, Middle Managers & Leadership Team

Steps 4 through 6 - Leadership Team

Steps 7 & 8 - Project Managers, Foremen, Superintendents, Supervisors, Middle Managers & Leadership Team

Step 9 - Leadership Team

Step 10 - Project Managers, Foremen, Superintendents, Supervisors, Middle Managers & Leadership Team

many people think they understand the rules of brainstorming, but it is worth taking a moment to review them.

- *State the problem in the form of a question.*

  Whenever possible, state the idea in the form of a question. How can we reduce raw material inventory from $2M to less than $750K? How can we reduce RFP response time from an average of five days to an average of one day?

- *Record all ideas on a flip chart and number them.*

  Have a skilled facilitator record all ideas on a flip chart and hang them all around the room.

- *Quantity of ideas is most important.*

  It is not uncommon to generate 100 or more ideas. Do not be concerned if there is a lull in the generation of ideas. Just wait for the ideas to come. Maybe take a break, get some fresh air, and start the process up again.

- *No criticism, discussion, or judgment allowed until all ideas have been presented. Clarification questions are okay.*

  This is a tough one and really requires a skilled facilitator. No one is to criticize someone else's idea—verbally or non-verbally. It is okay to ask clarifying questions so that the scope of the idea is understood, but do not analyze ideas at this time.

- *Encourage participation by all.*

  We encourage participation by all by going around the room in seating order so everyone gets a chance to put an idea on the flip chart. This prevents the more outspoken people in the room from dominating the meeting and allows the more reserved individuals to participate. Only one idea can be given per turn; if a person does not have an idea when it is his or her turn, the person just says "pass."

- *Piggyback—build on each other's ideas.*

  It is desirable to piggyback your idea off of someone else's, but you have to wait your turn.

- *Don't limit thinking or imagination—thinking "outside the box" is required here!*

  It is easier to tame down a wild idea than to build up a bland idea. Let your imagination run wild.

- *When all ideas have been presented, review each for feasibility and impact.*

The facilitator should begin to review the list of brainstormed ideas and lead the discussion on whether there are any ideas that are impractical. Maybe an idea would require too much capital, violate customer requirements, or be inconsistent with your overall strategies. If the entire group agrees that an idea is not practical at this time, then take it off the list or put it on a "Parking Lot" list for later consideration (and to make sure the ideas do not get lost). The goal is to whittle down the brainstormed lists to only feasible ideas. Remember, the team will ultimately vote on the best ideas in the final whittling.

Next, the brainstormed list is affinitized. In this step, similar ideas are consolidated or grouped together so that when the team votes for the best ideas in the next step, they will not use more than one vote to capture

Safety will always be our number-one priority and will be an integral part of everything we do.

one good idea. For example, remembering our previous discussion that 5S is a Lean tool that creates a safe, clean, and organized work area, suppose idea #37 was "creating a 5S plumbing materials cart to eliminate searching and hunting for plumbing materials could add 30 minutes per shift to tool time" and idea #93 was "use plumbing supplier managed inventory system to restock 5S plumbing materials cart, saving two hours of delay for five trades per week." Because these ideas are related, they would be grouped together.

Next, the team prioritizes the best ideas by voting. In multi-voting, each team member is given a set number of votes (usually 8-10% of the total number of feasible ideas) to use to vote for the ideas they think will have the greatest impact on achieving the goals established in Step 2. Limiting the number of votes requires the team to focus on the ideas with the greatest improvement potential from their perspective. The voting is done by secret ballot so as not to influence other people's opinions. The solutions with the greatest number of votes (ranked in order of number of votes) are the ideas the team will use to achieve the goals. Usually, the top 10-20 vote-getting ideas go forward from this point. At this time, the team will not know whether there are enough—or too many—ideas until they complete Step 6, the Reality Check. Step 6 can be an iterative step (check, adjust, and then check again).

Step 4—Define Parameters to Value Opportunities

The purpose of this step is to objectively evaluate the ideas and opportunities selected from the brainstorming. This valuation system must consider the following:

- The impact of the idea on the organization's goal(s)—also known as the idea "Benefit(s)"
- People resources required to implement the idea—also known as the idea "Effort"
- Capital expenditure required to fund the idea's implementation—"Effort"
- The risk that the idea cannot be implemented—"Effort"

At this point, the team is preparing to evaluate each idea by the potential "Benefit" versus the potential "Effort" involved to turn the brainstormed idea into a completed "project."

The first thing the team must do is take the company's goals (established in Step 2) and brainstorm what would be considered a low, medium, or high "project" impact for each goal. In this example, one of the goals is to improve operating income from 3% to 8% the following year. The question becomes "How much cost savings would need to be generated to support that level of operating income increase?" (Let's say that increase is $300,000). If the team decides that a project with an impact of $50,000 or higher would have a significant effect on operating income, then the team may establish ranges like the following:

- $0 to $20,000—low impact on operating income —score of 1
- $20,000 to $50,000—medium impact on operating income—score of 3
- Greater than $50,000—high impact on operating income—score of 5

10 Steps to Successful Policy Deployment

1. Establish a Mission and Behavioral Expectations
2. Develop Business Goals
3. Brainstorm for Opportunities to Achieve Goals
4. Define Parameters to Value Opportunities
5. Establish Weighting Requirements, Rate Opportunities, and Prioritize
6. Conduct a Reality Check
7. Develop Lean Implementation Plan
8. Develop Bowling Chart
9. Develop Countermeasures
10. Conduct Business Reviews

If the goal of improving operating income from 3% to 8% represented a $2 million increase, then the dollar impacts shown in the above example are probably too low. Team consensus is required here.

For each potential project, the team must establish low, medium, or high impact for each "Benefit" of a project. Once again, these benefits go back to the business goals of the organization. This process is a critical part of the planning process because it prevents the organization from working on the wrong projects or on the boss's "pet" project. It is the only way to take the "politics" out of the decisionmaking process.

The team must also establish low, medium, or high impact for each of the "Efforts" to complete each project. Generally, the "Effort" categories do not change. They consist of the estimated number of personnel and time required to complete a project, the estimated potential capital expenditure to complete a project, and the project risk. Of all the "Benefit" and "Effort" categories, the only one that is somewhat subjective is "Project Risk." Project Risk defines the probability that the project will not be completed or will not work when completed. All other categories must be definitively defined.

The completed Step 4 valuation parameters for these goals and projects (brainstormed ideas) look like this:

BENEFIT CATEGORIES TO ACHIEVING GOALS:

Net Income:
1 = Net Income impact of less than $25K
3 = Net Income impact of between $25K and $100K
5 = Net Income impact of greater than $100K

Cash Flow:
1 = $25K improvement in cash flow
3 = $25K to $50K improvement in cash flow
5 = Greater than $50K improvement in cash flow

Revenue Growth:
1 = Less than a 1% improvement in revenue growth
3 = 1% to 3% improvement in revenue growth
5 = Greater than a 3% improvement in revenue growth

EFFORT CATEGORIES— RESOURCES REQUIRED AND RISK

Resource Requirements:
1 = 240 or fewer people hours. For example, a one-week Kaizen Event with six people (not including preparation and follow-up work)
3 = 240 to 520 people hours
5 = More than 520 people hours

Capital Expenditure Requirements:
1 = Less than $25K
3 = Between $25K and $100K
5 = Greater than $100K

Project Risk
1 = Low
3 = Medium
5 = High

Ultimately, after Step 5, subtracting the Effort from Benefit will determine the project prioritization (Benefit – Effort = Prioritization). Naturally, we would like all projects to have a Benefit of a 5 and an Effort of a 1.

Step 5—Establish Weighting Requirements, Rate Opportunities, and Prioritize

The purpose of this step is to determine the importance weighting—or business necessitated priority—to assign to each of the Benefit and Effort categories. This is the final adjustment to the "Benefit – Effort" calculation so prioritization can occur.

This step is more critical than most people realize. Use the same three categories that were used in Step 4 under "Benefits": operating income, cash flow, and revenue growth. How the team "weights" each of these will have an impact on behaviors within the organization. Suppose the team establishes a weighting as follows:

30%	Operating Income
60%	Cash Flow
10%	Revenue Growth

What did the team communicate to the entire management team and the rest of the organization? That the organization should focus on anything that improves cash flow, such as reducing inventory, extending days payable, reducing days receivable, consolidating space (for example, eliminating the need for a warehouse), and reducing cycle times. People do not need to ask a lot of questions or seek permission. If they are not working on something to improve cash flow, they are working on the wrong thing. It does not mean that people are not going to do what they can to improve operating income. It does mean, that if confronted with two improvement initiatives—one that improves cash flow and another that will improve operating income—they should choose the project that will improve cash flow over everything else (except safety).

Likewise, the team needs to establish weighting criteria for the "Effort" side of the equation. The team needs to weight the importance of personnel requirements, capital expenditures, and project risk. Personnel requirements and capital expenditures are examples of an organization's resources that are not unlimited and may be available in an uneven supply. The amount of project risk a business can accept may reflect the organization's current financial position or its culture.

Effort weighting can prevent a project from reaching the final project recommended priority list when the organization is unable to support it from a resource or risk standpoint.

If the team establishes a weighting as follows:

20%	Personnel Requirements
70%	Capital Requirements
10%	Risk

then the team has just communicated to the rest of the company's associates that spending money on capital equipment or capital improvements is not desirable. Remember, Lean focuses on low cost or no cost solutions. It also communicates to the rest of the organization that the team is willing to take risks at this time and that people resources are available to complete projects.

10 Steps to Successful Policy Deployment

1. Establish a Mission and Behavioral Expectations
2. Develop Business Goals
3. Brainstorm for Opportunities to Achieve Goals
4. Define Parameters to Value Opportunities
5. Establish Weighting Requirements, Rate Opportunities, and Prioritize
6. Conduct a Reality Check
7. Develop Lean Implementation Plan
8. Develop Bowling Chart
9. Develop Countermeasures
10. Conduct Business Reviews

This information, along with the Step 4 valuation parameters, comprises the content of the spreadsheet known as the Impact Analysis Worksheet shown on the following page. (This and other templates are included in the referenced PD book previously mentioned.)

Note that the Total Benefit shown on the worksheet is calculated using the "weighted sum" of each benefit—likewise for the Total Effort. Also, the Project Descriptions shown on this spreadsheet are the nine ideas brainstormed and voted for in Step 3 of this example.

#	PROJECT DESCRIPTION	BENEFIT				EFFORT					
		Net Income	Cash Flow	Revenue Growth	TOTAL BENEFIT	Personnel Requirements	Capital Expenditure Requirements	Project Risk (Low, Medium, High)	TOTAL EFFORT	Benefit - Effort	RECOMMENDED PRIORITY
	Importance Weighting:	**30%**	**60%**	**10%**	**100%**	**20%**	**70%**	**10%**	**100%**		
1	Reduce System Cycle Time (from quote to cash) from 67 days to 30 days	5	5	5	**5.0**	3	1	1	**1.4**	3.6	***1***
2	Reduce returns from 3% of sales to less than 1% of sales	5	3	3	**3.6**	3	1	1	**1.4**	2.2	***3***
3	Reduce scrap in the foundry from 6% to 3% of sales	5	1	3	**2.4**	3	1	1	**1.4**	1.0	***4***
4	Reduce set-up time on machine #4 from 3 hours to less than 30 minutes	5	1	3	**2.4**	3	1	1	**1.4**	1.0	***5***
5	Reduce finished goods inventory from $9M to less than $3M	1	5	1	**3.4**	1	1	3	**1.2**	2.2	***2***
6	Consolidate warehouses after reducing finished goods inventory	3	1	1	**1.6**	3	1	1	**1.4**	0.2	***6***
7	Reduce pricing errors from 9 per order to zero	3	1	1	**1.6**	3	1	1	**1.4**	0.2	***7***
8	Reduce turnover of key personnel from 3% to zero	3	1	1	**1.6**	3	1	1	**1.4**	0.2	***8***
9	Develop a process to respond to an RFQ in a single phone call	1	1	5	**1.4**	3	3	1	**2.8**	-1.4	***9***

Figure 2.11
Impact Analysis Worksheet

Step 6—Conduct a Reality Check

Step 6 compares the value of all of the prioritized projects that the Leadership team has selected to work on in the current fiscal year (Step 5), when they are completed, to the organization's goals from Step 2.

The amount of project implementation time must also be considered here. A million dollar project is only worth $500,000 in the planning year if it takes six months to implement.

If the value of all the implemented projects meets or exceeds the organization's goals—congratulations! Move to Step 7. If they do not—read on.

This is the iterative part of Step 6. Check for goal attainment, make adjustments, and check again.

At this point, short of projects to meet the goals, the team has several options from which to choose for eliminating the shortfalls:

- Revisit the list of "voted for" ideas. Are there ideas that were not moved forward to Step 4 that would eliminate the shortfalls?
- Move the implementation timing forward in time for certain ideas so the results for the year are greater. This may require hiring additional resources (skilled Lean Facilitators) or relying on outside consultants. Using outside consultants would be necessary only until the organization trains internal candidates.
- Conduct another brainstorming session for the shortfall area.

- And as a last resort—revise the goal(s).

The following spreadsheet shows the nine projects from Step 5 successfully passing the reality check.

10 Steps to Successful Policy Deployment

1. Establish a Mission and Behavioral Expectations
2. Develop Business Goals
3. Brainstorm for Opportunities to Achieve Goals
4. Define Parameters to Value Opportunities
5. Establish Weighting Requirements, Rate Opportunities, and Prioritize
6. Conduct a Reality Check
7. Develop Lean Implementation Plan
8. Develop Bowling Chart
9. Develop Countermeasures
10. Conduct Business Reviews

	Project Descriptions that Support the High-Level Business Goals	Estimated Impact on Net Income	Estimated Impact on Cash Flow	Estimated Impact on Revenue Growth	Actual Impact on Net Income	Actual Impact on Cash Flow	Actual Impact on Revenue Growth
1	Reduce Total Cycle Time (from quote to cash) from 67 days to 30 days	$475,000	$200,000	$2,850,000			
2	Reduce returns from 3% of sales to less than 1% of sales	$175,000	$0	$350,000			
3	Reduce scrap in the foundry from 6% to 3% of sales	$210,000	$0	$0			
4	Reduce set-up time on machine #4 from 3 hours to less than 30 minutes	$185,000	$0	$0			
5	Reduce finished goods inventory from $9M to less than $3M	$60,000	$375,000	$0			
6	Consolidate warehouses after reducing finished goods inventory	$160,000	$0	$0			
7	Reduce pricing errors from 9 per order to zero	$145,000	$0	$0			
8	Reduce turnover of key personnel from 3% to zero	$105,000	$0	$0			
9	Develop a process to respond to an RFQ in a single phone call	$0	$0	$900,000			
10	Project 10	$0	$0	$0			
11	Project 11	$0	$0	$0			
12	Project 12	$0	$0	$0			
	Estimated Current Year Impact =	$1,515,000	$575,000	$4,100,000			
	Target =	$1,500,000	$500,000	$4,000,000			

Figure 2.12
Completed Reality Check

Step 7—Develop Lean Implementation Plan

The purpose of this step is to determine what Lean activities must be accomplished to support or enable the full implementation of the prioritized projects from Step 5 and who will be responsible for the activities.

The first things we list in the plan (see Figure 2.14, page 80) are the projects the team identified, valued, and prioritized in Steps 3 through 5. These are the projects the organization will resource with people and training to achieve the goals the Leadership Team developed in Step 2.

During the process of listing the identified projects, the team should make recommendations as to which Lean Tool should be used in the various projects. As illustrated in Figure 2.14, it was decided that Value Stream Mapping will be used to reduce Total Cycle Time from 67 days to 30 days in Project 1. A3 structured problem solving should be used to reduce scrap from 6% to 3% in Project 3, and so on.

At this point, it may seem confusing that we are asking the team to define which Lean Tools to assign to each project because we have only broadly discussed the Lean Tools at this point. Chapter 6 will define how to start the Lean Construction journey in an organization. It will give a step-by-step listing of when to start the training and Lean activities. It will show Policy Deployment as one of the first activities to complete, but only after the organization has been trained in a Lean Construction Overview session that discusses the Lean Construction Tools.

10 Steps to Successful Policy Deployment

1. Establish a Mission and Behavioral Expectations
2. Develop Business Goals
3. Brainstorm for Opportunities to Achieve Goals
4. Define Parameters to Value Opportunities
5. Establish Weighting Requirements, Rate Opportunities, and Prioritize
6. Conduct a Reality Check
7. Develop Lean Implementation Plan
8. Develop Bowling Chart
9. Develop Countermeasures
10. Conduct Business Reviews

The next part of Step 7 is to add the additional activities that need to be implemented first (usually from the Lean Culture or Lean Planning component areas) to properly support or enable the completion of the projects to be worked on by team members. These enabler activities generally only occur at the start of the Lean Construction journey and the first time the Policy Deployment plan is developed. Enablers communicate and prepare the organization for the journey ahead. Typical enabler activities include the following:

- Lean and/or Policy Deployment kickoff and announcement meetings
- Company-wide Lean training
- Countermeasures training (Step 9)
- Daily measurement systems to support Steps 7 and 8
- Owner, trade partner, and supplier meetings
- Development of company-wide communication systems to support teamwork (Chapter 3)
- Development of a monthly, all-associate meeting (The World Class standard is a meeting with the top leader in the facility at least monthly.)
- Train 1% of the company's people to be Certified Lean Facilitators

Once all the improvement projects and enabler activities are listed on the Lean Implementation Plan (Figure 2.14), it is time to determine the RACI (Responsible, Accountable, Consult, & Inform; Figure 2.13). We start out by identifying the one individual who will be held accountable for each activity.

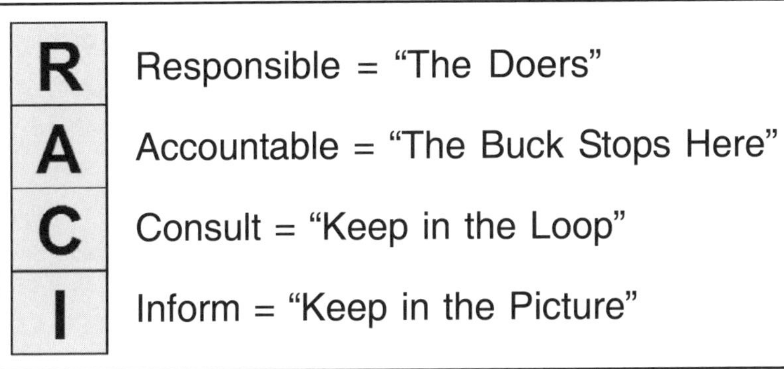

Figure 2.13

There can be only one name or set of initials under "Accountable," and it must be that of a member of the Leadership Team (Figure 2.14). Most likely more than one set of initials will appear in the "R" column (team "Responsible" for completing the activity). The "C" represents people we may need to "Consult" with to complete the action item. They may include personnel from Human Resources, IT, Finance, or Legal, as well as some external customer or supplier. The "I" indicates those people we need to keep "Informed" while completing the action item. Communication is important in everything an organization does before and during the journey to become World Class. It is extremely important that everyone understand what we are doing and WHY we are doing it!

The Accountable person and the Responsible team must create the timeline for their project's completion. All projects are implemented and completed using a team-based Kaizen Event format. Kaizen Events are activities in which the Responsible project team members spend 3-5 days (typically) in a full-time effort implementing their project. Team-based Kaizen Events are discussed in Chapter 4.

#	Lean Implementation Plan Projects which Support the High-Level Business Goals	Lean Tool	R	A	C	I	Status			
1	Reduce Total Cycle Time (from quote to cash) from 67 days to 30 days by the end of Q1	VSM	WCM, ck, pm, dd	LR	WCM	Leadership Team	25%	50%	75%	100%
2	Reduce returns from 3% of sales to less than 1% of sales by the end of Q1	Problem Solving	pm, ff, sr, dh	VF	Sales & Marketing	Leadership Team	25%	50%	75%	100%
3	Reduce scrap in the foundry from 6% to 3% of sales by the end of Q1	Problem Solving	WCM, dh, sr	MW	Suppliers	Leadership Team	25%	50%	75%	100%
4	Reduce set-up time on machine #4 from 3 hours to less than 30 minutes by the end of Q2	Set Up Reduction	dd, ck, hw	TD	Machine Manufacturers	Leadership Team	25%	50%	75%	100%
5	Reduce finished goods inventory from $9M to less than $3M by the end of Q2	Kanban Kaizen	WCM, pm, dh, pb, kl	PL	WCM	Leadership Team	25%	50%	75%	100%
6	Consolidate warehouses after reducing finished goods inventory by the end of Q3	Project	am, ck, ff, pz	PL	Accounting	Leadership Team	25%	50%	75%	100%
7	Reduce pricing errors from 9 per order to zero by the end of Q3	Problem Solving	pm, ff, pz, dh	LR	Sales & Marketing	Leadership Team	25%	50%	75%	100%
8	Reduce turnover of key personnel from 3% to zero by the end of Q4	Problem Solving	ff, pm, sr	AL	HR	Leadership Team	25%	50%	75%	100%
9	Develop a process to respond to an RFQ in a single phone call by the end of Q4	VSM & Process Cell Kaizen	WCM, am, ck	MW	IT	Leadership Team	25%	50%	75%	100%
	Additional activities that support the above Kaizen Events & the Lean Culture									
10	Improve hiring / recruiting / training / screening process		ck, pm, dd	LR	HR	Leadership Team	25%	50%	75%	100%
11	Conduct Policy Deployment rollout meeting & quarterly updates		pm, ff, sr, dh	VF	kr	Leadership Team	25%	50%	75%	100%
12	Provide Lean training for all associates		WCM, dh, sr	MW	WCM	Leadership Team	25%	50%	75%	100%
13	Form Leadership Team to implement office 5S (including training)		dd, ck, hw	TD	pl	Leadership Team	25%	50%	75%	100%
14	Clearly define and communicate Behavioral Expectations		pm, dh, pb, kl	PL	HR	Leadership Team	25%	50%	75%	100%
15	Develop skills matrix & cross-training plan		am, ck, ff, pz	PL	HR	Leadership Team	25%	50%	75%	100%
16	Cross-train to educate everyone on our Value Streams		pm, ff, pz, dh	LR	HR,td	Leadership Team	25%	50%	75%	100%
17	Implement Visual Management across facility		ff, pm, sr	AL	mw	Leadership Team	25%	50%	75%	100%
18	Create a "Sense of Urgency"		am, ck	MW	Executive staff	Leadership Team	25%	50%	75%	100%

Figure 2.14
Lean Implementation Plan

Step 8—Develop Bowling Chart

Step 7 shows timelines for completion of all the projects. Step 8 is a scoreboard that shows the results from completed projects, whether they are performing as planned, and how the completed projects are affecting the Step 2 business goals.

The scoreboard is referred to as a "Bowling Chart" (Figure 2.15). There are twelve months in a financial year and twelve frames in the game of bowling. The Bowling Chart will give the Leadership Team the ability to monitor progress toward the goals on a monthly basis and, as will be shown, the people responsible for each metric need to monitor progress on a daily basis. In this way the team can hold each other responsible and accountable for attaining the results.

The Bowling Chart, shown in Figure 2.15, has a listing of the high-level business goals (from the previous steps) and below them are the completed projects for which we are now measuring the results. The results of the projects then become the Key Performance Indicators (KPIs) for achievement of the business goals. The calendar months shown are for the organization's 12-month fiscal year (9 months have been cut-off in Figure 2.15).

10 Steps to Successful Policy Deployment

1. Establish a Mission and Behavioral Expectations
2. Develop Business Goals
3. Brainstorm for Opportunities to Achieve Goals
4. Define Parameters to Value Opportunities
5. Establish Weighting Requirements, Rate Opportunities, and Prioritize
6. Conduct a Reality Check
7. Develop Lean Implementation Plan
8. Develop Bowling Chart
9. Develop Countermeasures
10. Conduct Business Reviews

#	High-Level Business Goals & Key Performance Indicators (KPIs)	Owner	JOP	YTD		Jan	Feb	Mar
	High-Level Business Goals							
1	Achieve ZERO lost injury days for the next 12 months	MW	5	0	Plan	0	0	0
				0	Act	0	0	0
2	Improve Net Income from 3% to 8% of sales by the end of the fiscal year	LR	3.0%	3.0%	Plan	3.0%	3.0%	3.0%
				2.8%	Act	3.0%	3.2%	2.2%
3	Improve Free Cash Flow from 30% of net income to 70% of net income by the end of the fiscal year	VF	30.0%	30%	Plan	30%	30%	30%
				34%	Act	31%	34%	37%
4	Increase Revenue from $32 million to $36 million without eroding profits by the end of the fiscal year	LR	$32 M	$7.8	Plan	$2.6	$2.6	$2.6
				$8.1	Act	$2.6	$2.7	$2.8
	Key Performance Indicators (KPIs)							
5	Reduce System Cycle Time (from quote to cash) from 67 days to 30 days by the end of Q1	LR	67 days	54 days	Plan	67 days	50 days	45 days
				51 days	Act	67 days	47 days	40 days
6	Reduce returns from 3% of sales to less than 1% of sales by the end of Q1	VF	3.0%	3.0%	Plan	3.0%	3.0%	3.0%
				3.4%	Act	3.2%	3.0%	4.0%
7	Reduce scrap in the foundry from 6% to 3% of sales by the end of Q1	MW	6.0%	6.0%	Plan	6.0%	6.0%	6.0%
				5.8%	Act	5.8%	5.6%	6.0%
8	Reduce set-up time on machine #4 from 3 hours to less than 30 minutes by the end of Q2	TD	180 min	180	Plan	180	180	180
				180	Act	180	170	190
9	Reduce finished goods inventory from $9 million to less than $3 million by the end of Q2	PL	$9M	$8.67	Plan	$9.00	$9.00	$8.00
				$8.50	Act	$9.00	$8.50	$8.00
10	Consolidate warehouses after reducing finished goods inventory by the end of Q3 -- potential cost saving of $800K	PL	Project	$0.0	Plan	$0.0	$0.0	$0.0
				$0.0	Act	$0.0	$0.0	$0.0
11	Reduce pricing errors from 9 per order to zero by the end of Q3	LR	9	9	Plan	9	9	9
				7	Act	9	7	5
12	Reduce turnover of key personnel from 3% to zero by the end of Q4	AL	3.0%	3.0%	Plan	3.0%	3.0%	3.0%
				2.1%	Act	3.6%	0.0%	2.8%
13	Develop a process to respond to an RFQ in a single phone call by the end of Q4	MW	3 Days	3 Days	Plan	3 Days	3 Days	3 Days
				3 Days	Act	3 Days	3 Days	3 Days

= Project is at or above goal (Script A) (Discussed on page 86)
= Project is "RED" (below goal) and requires a countermeasure (Script B)

Figure 2.15
Bowling Chart

Every KPI must have an owner, and it should be a member of the Leadership Team. Under the column marked "Owner," put the initials of the individual who will be held accountable for that KPI during the monthly Business Review meetings of Step 10. This is the person who should be meeting with his/her project/Kaizen team on a daily basis and reviewing their metrics, which are displayed on daily charts and graphs in the area where the Kaizen Event or project took place. It is also this owner's responsibility to work with his/her team to develop immediate "countermeasures" (discussed in Step 9) if they see the KPI trending below their SMART goal. The owner and the team must be empowered to take immediate countermeasure action to put them back on target for achieving their SMART goal.

In addition to establishing the owner of each metric, the Leadership Team establishes the JOP or "Jumping Off Point" for each metric. (JOP = where will we end up based on the final measure of the previous year). Thus, if the goal is to improve our Net Income to 8%, we need to know what it is today—what our starting point is—3%. This measure is shown on the Figure 2.15 Bowling Chart.

The next part of Step 8 is to take the information or project timing that was developed during the Lean Implementation Planning process and determine when we can expect to see the results hitting our KPIs or the bottom line of our business. These are the numbers we insert in the row labeled "Plan" for each KPI. These numbers are month-to-month forecasted improvement numbers reflecting the project completions. They are not cumulative numbers. In the column labeled "YTD" (Year-To-Date), we insert the cumulative numbers for both the KPI plan and actuals for the year or accumulated results.

Step 9—Develop Countermeasures

The purpose of this step is to develop an understanding that the entire PD team must be taught how to implement countermeasures. Countermeasures are the Lean and Six Sigma tools that allow the project team(s) to make adjustments in their project implementation plan (Step 7) if they discover from their daily measurement system that they are below target. Countermeasure training allows the team(s) to own the project and operate autonomously. Countermeasure tools include the following:

- Team A3 Problem Solving (A3 template shown in Figure 2.16)
- Error Proofing
- Six Sigma DMAIC (Define, Measure, Analyze, Improve, Control)

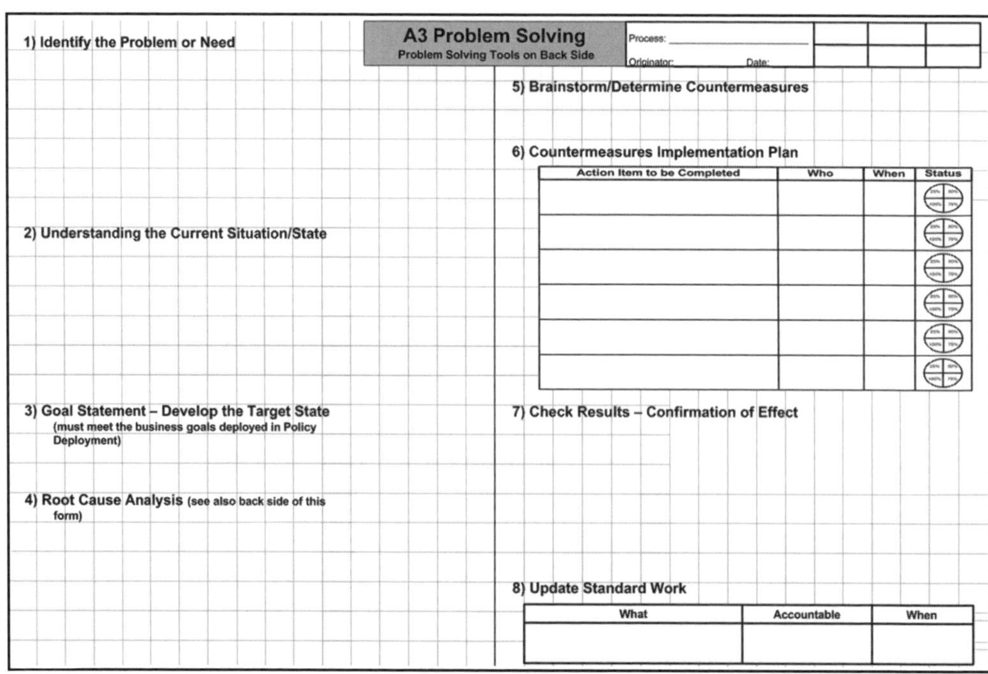

A3 Problem Solving
Problem Solving Tools on Back Side

Process: ____________
Originator: Date:

1) Identify the Problem or Need

2) Understanding the Current Situation/State

3) Goal Statement – Develop the Target State
(must meet the business goals deployed in Policy Deployment)

4) Root Cause Analysis (see also back side of this form)

5) Brainstorm/Determine Countermeasures

6) Countermeasures Implementation Plan

Action Item to be Completed	Who	When	Status

7) Check Results – Confirmation of Effect

8) Update Standard Work

What	Accountable	When

Figure 2.16
A3 Problem Solving Template

Ultimately, the goal of countermeasures training is to establish an environment in which the accountable people and the owners do not come to the Monthly Business Review meeting (Step 10) with problems but with solutions. They and their team have immediately identified a "below target" condition as a result of their daily measurements and have taken action.

The organization's Leadership Team is generally responsible for deciding what countermeasure training the associates should receive.

Step 10—Conduct Business Reviews

The purpose of the monthly Business Review meetings is to reiterate that the project implementation activities are on target to support achievement of the organization's goals.

This meeting is a review session of the Bowling Chart (Step 8), not a problem-solving meeting. Business Review meetings must be held monthly, like clockwork.

If good visual measurements and visual systems are in the workplace areas for the required activities of Step 7 and the goals of Step 8, then none of the monthly Business Review updates should be a surprise. Remember, good visuals mean that anyone should be able to walk through the organization and understand how everyone is progressing in terms of their goals without asking a question.

Conducting business reviews should be relatively simple. If this process is used religiously, people will come to monthly meetings prepared to present one of two scripts. Script "A" would indicate that a project metric is on track and is expected to stay on track.

SCRIPT A:

- It's on track.
- It'll stay on track.
- Any questions?

Script "B" would indicate that things are not necessarily going as planned. However, using this script means that the individual or team responsible for this project metric is monitoring it on a daily basis and using countermeasures to put a plan in place to correct the situation.

SCRIPT B:

- It's "X" weeks behind.
- The cause is "Y."
- The impact is "Z."
- Here's how and when we'll catch up.
- Any questions?

The Bowling Chart should be referred to in the monthly all-associate meetings. Such meetings are a signature activity of World Class Organizations. They give everyone an update on how the company is doing in terms of the goals. For this reason, the Bowling Chart review meeting should be held a couple of days before the monthly all-associate meeting. When not being updated or referenced, the Bowling Chart (an engineering plotter roll-size paper version) should be posted in a very visible area(s) of the organization.

Chapter Summary

"Beginning with the end in mind" means that Lean is implemented as an operating system in organizations. Lean has four components:

- Lean Planning
- Lean Concepts
- Lean Construction Tools
- Lean Culture

The four components must be implemented in parallel. The Policy Deployment activity meshes with the four components of Lean and works inside this operating system to link all Lean activities to the achievement of the organization's business goals.

To use Lean any other way ensures that the organization will make little or no progress with Lean.

References

AMI (Producer). (1999) *Joel Barker's Leadershift [DVD].*

Blanchard, D. (2007, October 1) Census of U.S. Manufacturers - Lean Green and Low Cost. *Industry Week.*

Covey, S. (1996) *The Seven Habits of Highly Effective People.* Provo, UT: Franklin Covey.

Crowley, M. and Domb, E. (1997) *Beyond Strategic Vision.* Boston: Butterworth-Heinemann.

Fayad, V. and Rubrich, L. (2009) *Policy Deployment and Lean Implementation Planning* (Rev. ed.). Fort Wayne, IN: WCM Associates LLC.

Haviland, W.A. (1987) *Cultural Anthropology* (5th ed.) New York, NY: Holt, Rinehart and Winston.

"Last Planner" is the Registered Trademark of the Lean Construction Institute, http://leanconstruction.org.

Larson, A. (2003) *Demystifying Six Sigma.* New York, NY: American Management Association.

Lean and Six Sigma are not leading to breakthroughs in corporate performance. (2011, September 30) *Manufacturing and Technology News*, vol 18, no 15.

Rubrich, L. & Watson, M. (2004) *Implementing World Class Manufacturing* (2nd ed.). Fort Wayne, IN: WCM Associates LLC.

Ryan, D. (n.d.) "The Wiremold Story" Powerpoint Presentation.

Shingo, S. (2007) *Kaizen and the Art of Creative Thinking.* Bellingham, WA: Enna Products Corporation.

Chapter 3

Developing a Lean Culture

With contributions by Vince Fayad

Fundamental Wiremold Company Premise

Companies are just collections (teams) of people trying to outperform other collections of people to satisfy a set of customers

The best, most motivated and focused team wins

Organizational culture is a learned process and is developed by the organization in response to the working environment established by the organization's leadership and management team.

Culture

Every organization or social group has a culture. It does not matter whether you are a for-profit or a not-for-profit organization. It does not matter whether you are in manufacturing, healthcare, construction, banking, or some other business—every social group has a culture. So what is culture?

To better understand what is meant by *culture*, let us explore several questions. What is culture? How do we acquire a culture? What purpose does a culture serve? Why would any culture change? How does this apply to corporate cultures?

What is culture? William A. Haviland in his textbook, *Cultural Anthropology* defines it as follows:

> Culture: A set of rules and standards shared by members of a society, which when acted upon the members, produce behavior that falls within a range the members consider proper and acceptable.

How do we acquire a culture? Culture is a learned process. We begin to learn our culture from our mother and father, aunts and uncles, brothers and sisters, and our extended family. We learn what is right and what is wrong. We learn what behavior is acceptable and what behavior is unacceptable. Eventually, this knowledge is extended into the community. We continue to learn our culture from friends, teachers, a religious cleric, maybe from a law enforcement agent. We continue to learn our culture which is reflected in our behavior.

> All culture is learned rather than biologically inherited. One learns one's culture by growing up

> with it. Ralph Linton referred to culture as humanity's "social heredity." The process whereby culture is transmitted from one generation to the next is called enculturation. Through enculturation one learns the socially appropriate way of satisfying one's biological determined needs. It is important to distinguish between the needs themselves, which are not learned, and the learned ways in which they are satisfied. The biological needs of humans are the same as those of other animals: food, shelter, companionship, self-defense, and sexual gratification. Each culture determines in its own way how these needs will be met. (Haviland, 1987)

What purpose does a culture serve? If our culture guides our behavior and allows us to meet our biological needs, then our culture helps us SURVIVE in the environment in which we live and work. *Survival* is a very strong word. Without a shared culture, everyone in a society would act or behave differently. No one would be able to anticipate someone else's behavior, and no one would understand why people behave the way they do. Life would be very chaotic. Biological needs would not be met and eventually the society would either adapt or die!

> A culture cannot survive if it does not satisfy certain basic needs of its members. The extent to which a culture achieves the fulfillment of these needs will determine its ultimate success. "Success" is measured by the values of the culture itself rather than by those of an outsider. A culture must provide for the production and distribution of goods and services considered necessary for life. It must provide for biological continuity through the

> reproduction of its members. It must acculturate new members so that they can become functioning adults. It must maintain order among its members. It must likewise maintain order between members and outsiders. Finally, it must motivate its members to survive and engage in those activities necessary for survival. (Haviland, 1987)

If you want to change the culture in your organization—then you have to manage or change the environment!

Why would any culture change? Culture is a learned process that aids us in meeting our biological needs and helps us survive in the environment in which we live and work. If the environment changes, then the culture would have to change to increase the chances of its members surviving. Notice we say "increase" our chances of surviving. There are no guarantees in life. The more flexible and adaptable a culture is to an ever-changing environment, the greater chance it has in adapting or responding to environmental pressures.

> All cultures change over a period of time, although not always as rapidly or as massively as many are doing today. Changes take place in response to such events as environmental crises, intrusion of outsiders, or modification of behavior and values within the culture. (Haviland, 1987)

How does this apply to corporate cultures? Organizations are no different from any social group. They have their own language, and people learn the culture of the organization from the very first day they start their jobs—sometimes even sooner. They learn what behavior is acceptable and what behavior is unacceptable.

They learn the organization's culture from their supervisor (parent), they learn it from other associates in their department (siblings), and they learn it from other associates in the organization (extended family). People learn their "place" in the organization, their role and responsibility. They learn what behavior management expects from them.

When asked, most organizations will tell you that their culture has changed over the last five to ten years and that their culture will most likely change again over the next five to ten years. If that is the case, why would any organization leave this culture change to chance? Why would you not determine the culture you want in your organization and put a plan into place to make it happen?

Has the environment changed in the construction industry? Just refer to the *Introduction*—the Chinese, as well as other foreign competitors, are establishing construction companies inside the United States. If the environment out there is changing, then the construction industry must change to survive. What is the definition of insanity? Doing the same thing over and over again and expecting a different result! Are we insane? Are we willing to do what it takes to make the necessary changes so we can successfully compete with anyone who threatens our industry?

Culture development begins with the creation of "guiding principles" or "behavioral expectations" as part of the Policy Deployment activity in Lean Planning. Because the principles and expectations are developed in Lean Planning by the organization's Leadership Team, they set the cultural framework.

You Change the Culture by Changing the Environment

When Bob Ayers became president of Sulzer Pumps in Portland, Oregon, the company was losing $16M dollars a year on about $200M dollars in sales. The company also had an on-time delivery performance of 49%, and most of their customers would not even allow them to quote a job anymore. According to an external consultant that they hired to survey their customers, there was "no such thing as a good pump company; you are all bad. But of all the pump companies, Sulzer was the worst."

Bob Ayers started by changing the environment. He instituted monthly, mandatory all-associate meetings. He shared all financial data at these meetings in a clear, concise manner. He would then open up the meeting for questions. He always stated that he would give people an honest answer—they may not like his answer, but they would get a brutally honest response. He would measure the quality of these monthly meetings by how many tough questions were asked. The entire Leadership Team was required to be at these monthly meetings to answer questions as well. If they could not answer a question, they wrote it down and always got back to people with an answer.

Bob continued to change the environment by putting the Leadership Team's mission, vision, goals, and behavioral expectations on a one-page transparency that he showed at every meeting he attended. He had Human Resources set up weekly "Coffee with the President" meetings. H.R. was expected to randomly select 12 people throughout the company from as many different disciplines as possible and invite them to have coffee and donuts with him. Bob knew that there were most likely people in the company who were afraid to ask questions in the monthly meetings, and he wanted to know what was going through people's minds. He would start out each meeting with his one-page transparency (mission, vision, goals, and behavioral expectations) and then open the meeting up for questions. The meetings were very lively and successful.

Bob did not stop there. They were in a critical situation, and he had to turn the company around fast. He then joined the company's basketball team, he had H.R. start a special team to focus on community projects [Special Olympics, Habitat for Humanity, etc.], and they started to have barbecue lunches for all associates on every shift, every time they achieved one of their goals. The entire Leadership Team was expected to be out there flipping hamburgers for their people to show their appreciation.

Bob did many things to change the environment throughout Sulzer Pumps. He did "Management by Walking Around," and he knew everyone on a first name basis. As a result, Sulzer Pumps went from a negative $16M to being one of the most profitable companies within the Sulzer Group. Their on-time delivery performance went to 100% for all their standard products, and they were sole-sourced by many of the companies that would not let them quote jobs 5 years earlier.

It takes time to change a culture. But the only way to change the culture is by changing the environment!

— Vince Fayad

Leadership, Communication, Empowerment, and Teamwork

There are four elements that can be used to fill in the cultural framework and affect culture change in an organization: leadership, communication, empowerment, and teamwork.

Lean is all about creating a common language and a common culture in your organization. It provides an environment for people with different backgrounds, experiences, educational levels, and skills to work together for a common good.

Leadership

All organizations have a culture (positive or negative) that is developed, formed, and modified over years based on the actions, examples, and behavioral model presented by the Leadership Team to the rest of the organization.

Unfortunately, the responsibility and accountability for the development of a positive organizational culture must be missing from CEO, COO, president, and plant manager job descriptions because culture development is most often set adrift to develop on its own at the supervisory level. Because many supervisors, brought up through the organization, were trained (and still are) in a "command and control" mindset, a negative culture is developed.

When the organization is not performing well, the Leadership Team then blames all the people, who they say have "bad attitudes" and "don't care about the company."

We were recently asked to attend a Leadership Team meeting at a company that was having difficulty sustaining the implementation of Lean within their organization. While we sat around the conference table discussing the symptoms, a floor supervisor, who had only been with the company four to five months, spoke up. "The problem with this company is the people—they all have bad attitudes and they don't care." In pursuing this discussion, we asked the Director of H.R. if they were hiring people with "bad attitudes." The H.R. Director assured the team that the H.R. screening processes brought in good people, a point no one on the team disagreed with. We then asked the Leadership Team to consider how good employees turned into employees with bad attitudes who didn't care about the company after a few years of exposure to the environment (culture) that the Leadership Team had created in the organization. Embarrassed by recognizing the truth in these discussions, the Leadership Team quickly refocused their efforts on how they could create an environment in which good people could excel.

After a “root cause” examination of this good employee to bad-attitude employee transformation, cultural elements that would prevent a successful Lean implementation are found:

- People are told to use their arms and legs to do their job—not their brains.
- They are not asked for their ideas, only told what to do.
- They are not trained in anything other than by OJT (on-the-job training).
- They are not asked to participate in securing the company’s (and their) future.
- While they are told they are on the “team,” no one communicates with them other than to place blame.

The Top 3 Reasons Lean Implementations Fail

1) Lack of Top Management Leadership and Support

2) Lack of Communication

3) Lack of Middle Management/ Supervisor Buy-In

As has been noted previously, the Leadership Team can jump-start the culture change process by issuing organizational behavioral expectations. It should be understood that behavioral expectations will only produce culture change if they are modeled by the Leadership Team. Because the culture change process can take years, the Leadership Team must be committed to the guidelines as a new way of doing business.

As discussed in Chapter 2, one of the most important characteristics of a good leader is to provide a mission/ vision for where the organization is going to be one, three, and five years down the road and a map of how to get there. Joel Barker defines a "leader" in his video, *Leadershift*, as "Someone you choose to follow to a place you would not go by yourself!" He goes on to say that the role of a leader is to find, recognize, and secure the future. So the real question is whether or not the people in your organization TRUST you enough to follow you to a place they would not go by themselves. It is up to every leader to develop a trustful, respectful, and mutually beneficial relationship with his or her people. This relationship includes the communication to and the motivation of the organization to implement the mission/vision.

Once you have developed this relationship, it is then your role as a leader to find, recognize, and secure the future of your organization. You then need to define this "place" where people "would not go to by themselves." The next step is to put a plan in place to secure the future. These steps can all be accomplished using the 10 Step Policy Deployment process (Chapter 2). Having a plan is only part of the equation. If no one knows where your organization is going or how you are going to get there, then they will not trust you to follow you to this new place they would not go to on their own. Communication, Communication, Communication!

Additionally, good leaders must be able to communicate and motivate the organization to implement the vision.

Developed by Vita Learning, the "Four Absolutes of Leadership" are very simplistic on the surface, but are extremely profound, powerful concepts and principles that leaders can use to communicate and motivate.

FOUR ABSOLUTES OF LEADERSHIP

1. Maintain Self-Esteem
2. Focus on Behavior
3. Encourage Participation
4. Listen to Motivate and Communicate

1. **Maintain Self-Esteem:** Self-esteem generally refers to an individual's sense of self-worth. Whenever we attack someone's self-worth, only one of two things will happen: he/she will either fight back or run away and hide. We call this the "fight or flight" syndrome.

   Nothing beneficial or constructive ever comes from either of these situations. It is important to understand what we do to enhance one person's self-esteem may or may not work for someone

Whenever we attack someone's self-worth, only one of two things will happen: he/she will either fight back or run away and hide. We call this the "fight or flight" syndrome.

else. The converse is also true: what damages one person's self-esteem may or may not damage someone else's self-esteem. Every individual is different. We must get to know people on a personal level to really understand how our actions affect other people. Leaders must maintain people's self-esteem regardless of the situation.

Wherever you are—at the jobsite supervising a crew, in the office with a team planning your next project, or in the shop fabricating necessary duct work—you must always be cognizant of how you interact with people and do what is necessary to maintain or enhance people's self-esteem. It may be nothing more than walking up to someone and shaking their hand and thanking them for taking care of the customer in your absence.

As soon as we observe a behavior, we make an inference about that behavior. Doing so is normal and natural—the key is we should never act on our inference; we must act on the behavior.

2. **Focus on Behavior:** This absolute ties nicely into our discussions of behavioral expectations and is a key leadership principle. It is also the most difficult for leaders to understand. The key issue is that, as soon as we observe a behavior, we make an inference about that behavior. Doing so is normal and natural. The key is we should never act on our inference; we must act on the behavior. For example, if we know someone came to work late three times the previous week, we may infer that the person is lazy, has a bad attitude, and does not care about the job. When we approach this person about the tardiness, we may get upset and tell the person they have a bad attitude. We have attacked their self-esteem and violated the first principle of leadership. This person may fire back and attack or run away and hide. No good will come from this scenario.

However, if we approach the individual and state the observable behavior—"I observed you coming to work late three times last week, what is going on?"—, we may get a completely different response or reaction. We may learn that the person has an ailing parent who needs assistance first thing in the morning. We may also learn that the person stays late every evening to make sure the team does not suffer from the tardiness. Or we may learn that the person does have a bad attitude.

A leader is in the most powerful position when he or she has firsthand, observable information.

A leader is in the most powerful position when he or she has firsthand, observable information. Never rely on secondhand information. Stay focused on the behavior, good or bad, and do not act on your inferences.

3. **Encourage Participation:** This absolute fits neatly into our leadership principle of empowerment. Do not solve problems or provide solutions for your people. In the above example, we may find that the person is just having problems getting organized in the morning so they can be at work on time. A good leader may probe and investigate what they think should be done to rectify the situation. The response could be explored and an action plan put in place. It would then be necessary to follow up on the agreed-upon action plan.

Good leaders listen more than they speak.

4. **Listen to Motivate and Communicate:** Good leaders listen more than they speak. Leaders know that they will never learn anything if they are doing all the talking. Learning to listen to the voices of your customers, processes (your people), and your suppliers will enhance people's self-esteem and promote communication.

When you really focus on someone and actively listen to what they have to say, you are communicating that you value their opinion. This action, in turn, enhances people's self-esteem.

Summary of Lean Leadership Concepts:

√ People are basically good—they want to do the right thing.

√ Company associates will only be as good as their leaders.

√ The Leadership Team should establish organizational behavioral expectations and values.

√ When problems in an organization occur (i.e., safety, scrap, poor quality, low productivity, etc.), 98 percent of them are a result of the organization's systems—not people.

√ It is the Leadership Team's responsibility to create an environment and organizational systems in which it is easier for company associates to be successful than to fail.

√ Support for change requires trust—trust requires great two-way communication.

√ With trust, a vision, and a plan to achieve that vision, company associates have unlimited capacity for change.

√ Leaders make hard things easy—not easy things hard.

√ System thinking is required.

√ As the Leadership Team, there can be no individual winners or losers—you win as a team or lose as a team.

Communication

There is no teamwork in any organization without great two-way communication. When Leadership Teams are surveyed, 99 percent say that teams and teamwork are important to the success of their organization. Yet these same organizations have few, if any, successful teams. Establishing teams—easy to say, but hard to do! Or is it?

Great two-way communication is the ongoing investment a Leadership Team must make in its people

There are four elements required for teamwork to develop in any organization:

1) High levels of two-way communication

2) Team members with diverse backgrounds

3) Common purpose/motivated by mission

4) Common goals and measurements

While Leadership Teams "mouth" the need for teams and teamwork, their actions against these requirements indicate something different.

For a team to develop and be successful, everyone in the organization must have a copy of the playbook. This is the importance of doing the 10 Step Policy Deployment process. This deployment process, like a team playbook, outlines the organization goals (win the Super Bowl) and the activities (plays) that the team must execute to achieve the goals. The team has measurement systems (scoreboard) to track progress. The Leadership Team (quarterback and coaches) are constantly communicating verbally and visually with the team and sub-team members (offensive line, defense, special teams, etc.). The team makes adjustments along the path to the goal. One can only imagine the results of a football play in which the quarterback only communicates the "play call" to two team members instead of all ten in the huddle. However, this is most often the norm for Leadership Teams in American business.

Based on our experience, running many organizations from the general manager and plant manager level, we have learned and believe that 98 percent of people in organizations want to take care of their customers, they want the company to be successful, and they want to have jobs at the company in the future. To access these resources, an environment (culture) must be created in which these 98 percent know they are valuable members of the team. The question for Leadership Teams and managers is the following: Do you want six to eight managers trying to achieve the company's budget, plans, and goals, or do you want the entire organization doing that?

If Lean is the engine to becoming a World Class Enterprise, then communication is the fuel.

Without this Leadership Team communication, people in most organizations will learn about what is going on through the "rumor mill." Change is discovered, not announced. Remember, a rumor's sole purpose in life is to fill voids in communication. Generally, the rumor mill is the most reliable way of obtaining information when the Leadership Team fails to effectively communicate. People know when change is in the wind. They see management going to off-site meetings and getting involved in different types of training. Managers and supervisors come back from these events speaking a different language and acting differently. If management does not effectively communicate the vision for the future and the impact that change is going to have on the organization and the people, then confusion and rumors ensue (as depicted in the model shown below).

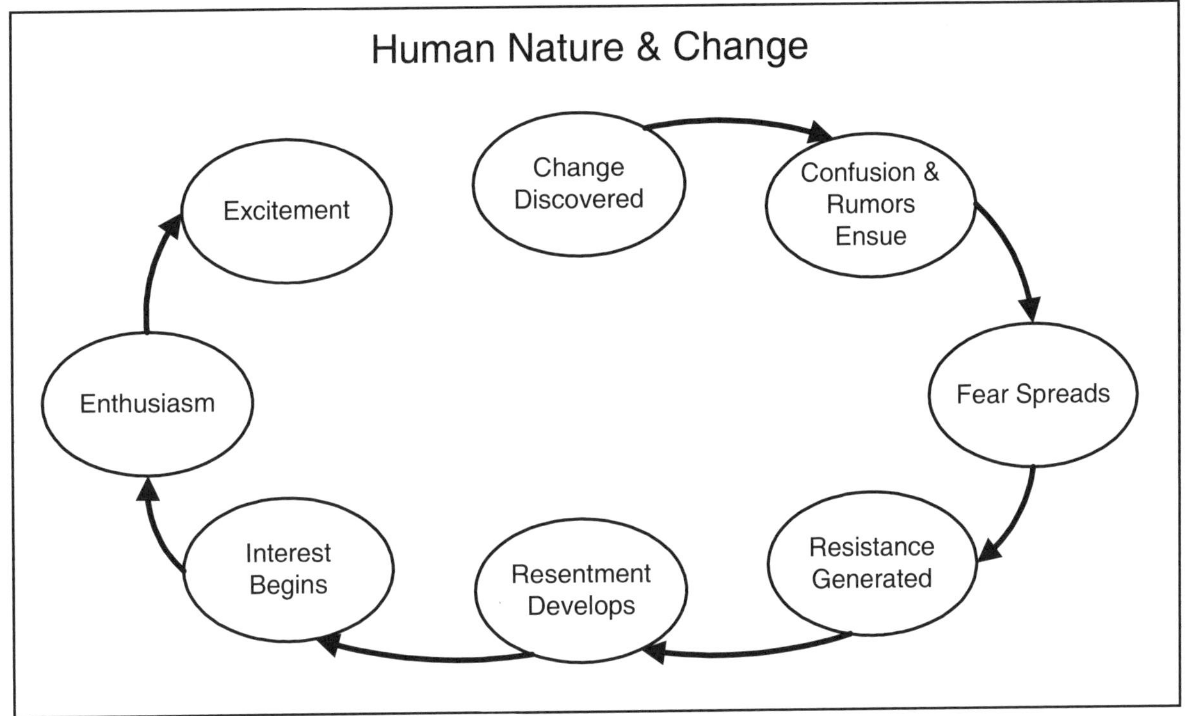

Figure 3.1
Human Nature and Our Reaction to Uncommunicated Change

Confusion and rumors begin to spread fear in the organization and resistance begins to develop. It now takes a great deal of effort to change or overcome the resentment that has set in. In some organizations, management is never able to change or recover from the resentment that has occurred. Figure 3.1 repeats itself every time a change is discovered and not announced.

An effective Leadership Team can short circuit this confusion, fear, resistance, and resentment loop by announcing a change and communicating it to everyone at the same time. Then by communicating, communicating, and communicating about the change, the Leadership Team can begin to develop interest from the organization in the change (see Figure 3.2). The Leadership Team must continue to grow this interest, enthusiasm, and excitement through ongoing communication updates to the vision and the plan for what the organization will look like one, three, and five years down the road.

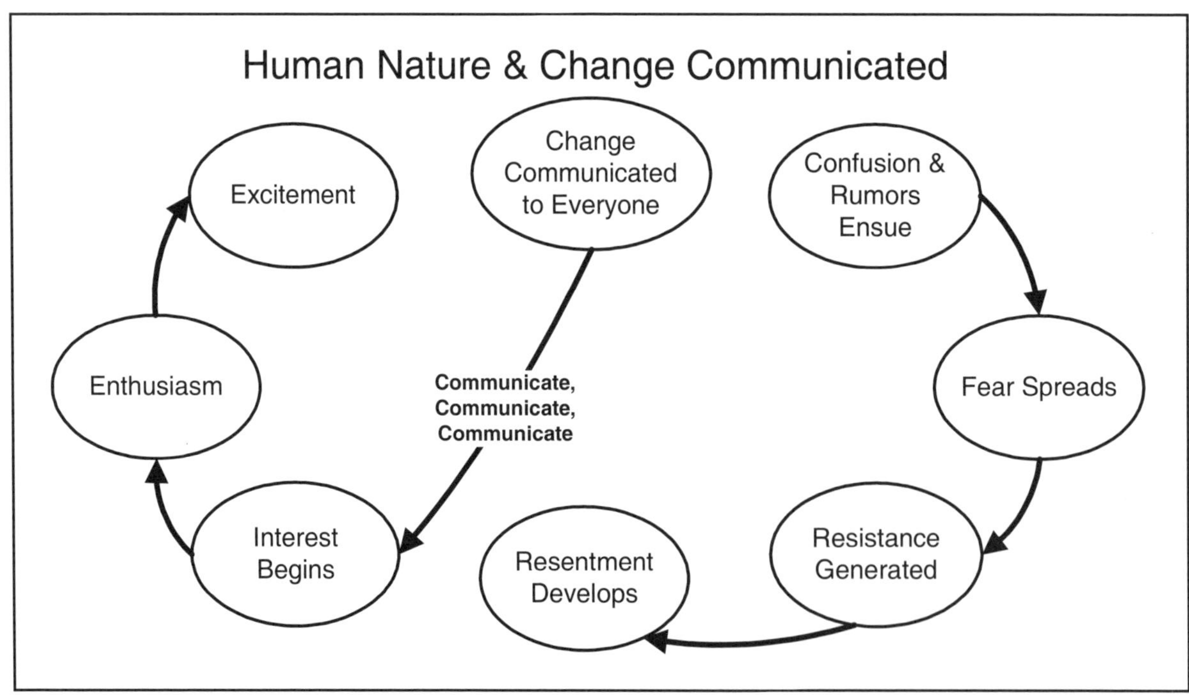

Figure 3.2
Human Nature with Change Communicated

It is important to remember that the communication from all Leadership Team members must be honest and consistent. When the Leadership Team "breaks the huddle," every team member must be reading from the same page. Leadership Team trust violations will greatly impede or destroy the Lean deployment effort. The organization is not expecting the Leadership Team to be perfect (mistake-free), but it is expecting the team to be honest.

> Several years ago we were helping a small organization (<100 people) implement Lean. We spent extra time working with the Leadership Team because, in our initial organizational assessment, lack of trust in the Leadership Team came out in our interviews with company associates. The company associates wanted to help improve the company, but were hesitant to believe the Leadership Team was actually prepared to start "doing things differently." Presented with a summary of the assessment concerns, the Leadership Team assured us that they were prepared to follow the organization's new code of conduct so the necessary culture change would be supported. This was related to all the company associates in a Lean Kick-off meeting.
>
> Several months later, it was Christmas time. The president of the organization wanted to send some wine across state lines to a colleague via UPS. The shipping clerk informed the president that doing so was illegal (at the time). The president told the shipping clerk to lie and send it anyway. Within 20 minutes, this story spread throughout the entire facility, reinforcing the workforce's lack of trust in the Leadership Team. The Lean implementation died, and three years later, it is still dead.

Summary of Lean Communication Concepts:

√ A lack of communication in an organization supports all 8 types of business waste.

√ Rumors start due to a lack of communication, and they negatively affect morale, productivity, and culture.

√ Teamwork does not exist without great two-way communication.

√ Leaders must tell the entire team what the play is and then frequently update that information (the quarterback in the huddle analogy).

√ Communication can be a simple thing if it is done on a regular basis—make it a part of the Leadership Team's daily routine.

√ "All hands" team communication updates must occur monthly (at a minimum).

√ Remember the advertising axiom that people fully understand a communication only after they have seen and/or read it at least four times. Use multiple platforms for your communications (newsletters, bulletin boards, check stuffers, etc.).

√ Effective communication includes both verbal and visual communication.

√ Communication and information transfer effectiveness must be measured (see the H.R. section on page 115).

Empowerment

Most people have a real misconception of empowerment. They think they can just tell people they are empowered and they should just get on with their jobs. This is not empowerment; it is abdication. All four of these components must work together: Leadership, Communication, Empowerment, and Teamwork, and they must work in this order.

The most important resource an organization has is its people!!

Empowerment is not something we do to another person. The best we can do, as leaders, is to provide an environment in which empowerment can occur. Leaders cannot just announce or proclaim that people are now empowered. They must be proactive in establishing an environment conducive to an empowered workforce. Here are the cultural elements of an empowering environment:

- Associates are recognized as the organization's most valuable resource.
- Teamwork is used throughout the organization.
- Decisionmaking is delegated.
- Openness, initiative, and risk taking are promoted.
- Accountability, credit, responsibility, and ownership are shared. (Here *ownership* means psychological ownership of their job responsibilities and work area, not stock certificate ownership.)

Once the team members know what part of the play (from the playbook) or what role they must fill for the team to be successful, empowerment allows them to use 100 percent of their creativity, skills, and knowledge in doing their job without fear of retribution or second guessing by management.

This is what an empowered workforce looks and works like:

- Associates have been trained and cross-trained so they know and understand their daily work assignments.
- Associates have been given daily, weekly, and monthly goals and have the ability to measure progress towards those goals.
- Associates know and understand where the organization is going and how they are going to get there.
- Associates take care of the present, allowing the leaders to focus on the future.

It is important to understand that associate empowerment is an evolutionary process, not a revolutionary one.

Summary of Lean Empowerment Concepts:

√ To empower your people, you must trust them; to trust them, you must develop them; so Lean is all about developing your people!

√ You can empower a well-trained, cross-functional, and disciplined workforce only after they know and understand where the organization is going and how they are going to get there.

√ Empowerment is the cultural response of the workforce to the Leadership Team's creation of an empowering environment.

√ Empowerment is an evolutionary process—not a revolutionary one.

√ The goal of empowerment is to develop a company of Leaders.

Teamwork

With the primary requirement for teamwork to occur—communication and the empowerment evolution that follows—in place, it is now possible to close the loop on the three remaining elements (from page 103):

1) High levels of two-way communication

2) Team members with diverse backgrounds

3) Common purpose/motivated by a mission

4) Common goals/measurements

The second requirement is diversity. The most creative, best problem-solving teams are those with team members who have diverse backgrounds. Diversity allows the composite team to view problems and opportunities from many angles or facets—a 360 degree global view. Every person working on a problem sees the problem from his or her angle, facet, or frame of reference. This angle is determined by the person's background, education, experiences, and culture (BEEC). These factors force a person to view the problem from that angle or frame of reference. If there are 10 people on a team and they all have similar BEEC factors (or think of it as 9 clones of the same person), great or even good creativity or problem solutions will not occur because the problem or opportunity is not seen in its entirety. Will the team with similar BEECs come up with a solution? Yes. Will it ultimately be viewed as a good solution? No. This poor solution is strictly the result of the non-diverse team not being able to take a global view of the problem and, therefore, being unable to problem solve for all aspects and potential complexities of the problem.

American organizations have a mixed bag in terms of diversity. Fortune 1000 firms that work and compete in the global economy first learned that diversity was required to do business globally. They then learned that this diversity brought power to their teams. However, for companies of 500 people or less, which represent greater than 95 percent of all American businesses, it's a different story. When the President, CEO, or plant manager of these organizations is asked whether the organization has diversity in its workforce, the answer will be yes. True enough, but there is no power (only untapped power) in this type of diversity. This diversity is based on hiring members of one or more local ethnic groups who will work for the wages being paid. In general, English communication skills are not a job requirement. Without communication, there is no teamwork, and therefore, no "diversity power." The largest type of waste (of the eight types of waste) in these organizations is #8—underutilized human resources.

Ultimately, the goal of team diversity, regardless of whether it is ethnic, cultural, or social, is to develop a team that is unencumbered by "group think" but can effectively communicate and in due course develop team consensus.

Required elements #3 (common purpose/motivated by a mission) and #4 (common goals and measurements) are usually addressed together. The largest barrier to these two elements is departmentalization. Departmentalization blocks businesses from achieving organizational wide teamwork for the following reasons:

- Departmentalization usually means individual departmental goals. Individual department goals prevent teamwork throughout the organization because everyone is concerned about achieving their own department's goals and how they will affect their own performance reviews and merit pay increases.

- These individual department goals also produce a lack of Lean "system thinking." The system is broadly defined as the processes required from the time an RFP is received until the project is delivered. For owner satisfaction to occur, everyone in the organization must have owner satisfaction as a common goal so they will all pull in the same direction. System thinking requires that all decisions and improvements in an organization are made based on their impact on the system efficiency. If a suggestion will improve department efficiency but will negatively affect the system efficiency, it is not done.

  For example, people working for a department (instead of the system) generally process the "information product" passing through their department in production batches. They use batch production because, for their department, batching is most efficient (due to mental or physical setup time). Unfortunately, batching stops the information product flow, extending the information product lead time and making the system less efficient. Additionally, these individual department goals may cause other behaviors detrimental to system efficiency, for example, the business development manager who cares only about "getting the project" and not making sure that all the owner's expectations and requirements are clearly defined, or engineering tossing a design "over the wall" to the subcontractor even though the design is not installation ready.

- Departmentalization inhibits cross-training, which prevents associate growth. It limits the full use of our mental resources in improving the system efficiency because few people understand how the system operates.

Lean drives down the authority, responsibility, and accountability to the lowest levels in the organization. It includes eliminating silos and departmentalization that are a traditional part of most corporate cultures so the flow of information and material through the organization can improve. An organization that is organized in silos or departments creates many handoffs. Wherever there are handoffs, there are delays and opportunities for errors.

In a World Class organization, flexible, cross-functional teams are created to focus on processes that provide products or services to particular customers or markets from RFP to project delivery. These Value Streams or Business Units are assigned to a team leader who forms a team. The team is then given the autonomy to manage its own processes based on the organizational goals. The teams are focused on maximizing the amount of value delivered to the owner.

Summary of Lean Teamwork Concepts:

√ Lean business is a team sport.

√ All organizational and area (department) improvements must have a positive impact on the system efficiency.

√ The workforce must have clear goals with metrics in place so they can measure their progress.

√ Powerful teams are diverse teams.

√ Common goals and a common mission keep everyone pulling in the same direction.

Human Resources' Role in Developing a Lean Culture

A wise corporate president once said it was okay to make mistakes as long as you learn from them and do not repeat them in the future. But he also went on to say that there are two mistakes managers or leaders could make that are difficult to recover from; they are decisions about capital investments and people. People are any organization's most important asset and the key to its success.

Unfortunately, most organizations do not fully utilize H.R. in the company culture-building activity. The company culture is left adrift to develop on its own, and Human Resources is relegated to hiring, firing, and keeping us legal. Have you ever seen any Certified Lean Facilitators that have come from H.R.?

In Lean, the H.R. area plays an extremely vital role in establishing Lean as "the way we run our business." H.R. closes the feedback loop on the people side between "the strategy, culture, and plan we say we are deploying" and the actual deployment.

An important part of this loop closure includes integrating Lean measures (support and participation in Lean activities, as well as adherence to behavioral expectations) into the following traditional H.R. areas:

- Performance appraisals
- Candidates for promotion
- Merit increases
- Hiring recommendations
- New employee training
- Bonus incentives

The first time the organization promotes or publicly rewards someone who is less than a 100 percent supporter of Lean activities, it sends a messages to the organization that effectively dooms the Lean deployment.

As mentioned in Chapter 2, defining a company's culture adds an aspect of "how" people do their jobs. It adds a new dimension to individual or team performance evaluations that typically measure only performance—"what" they did. The typical performance review is one dimensional—performance only, as shown on the chart below. Within this one dimensional evaluation, there are levels of unacceptability and acceptability.

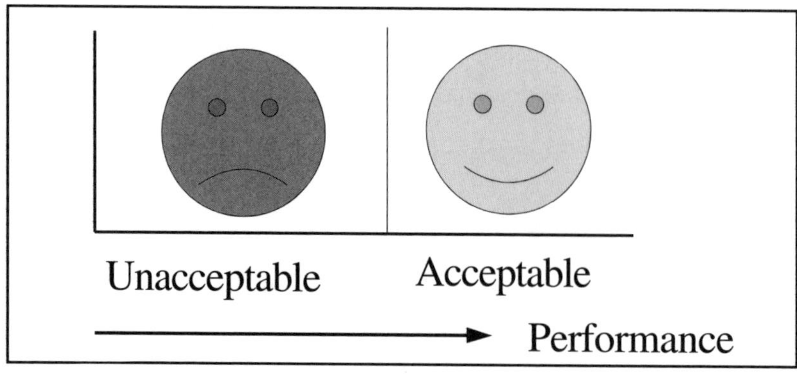

Figure 3.3
Typical Associate Evaluation

In this one dimensional measure, we can confusingly lump together two different types of acceptable or higher performers. The individual who is getting acceptable performance using communication, empowerment, and teamwork within his or her work group and the person who is getting acceptable performance using fear, intimidation, and a command and control style of management. Only when the "how" of culture measure is added to the evaluation does the separation in types of performers occur as shown in the following figure:

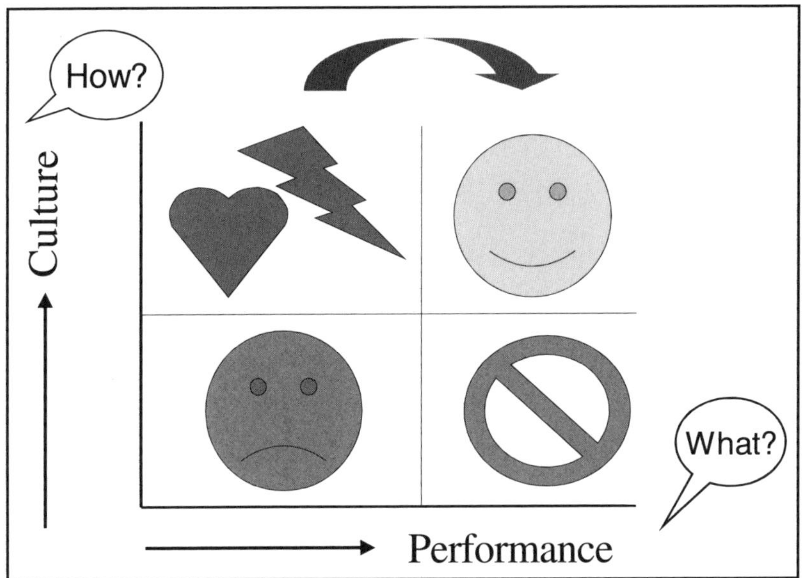

Figure 3.4
Culture and Performance Associate Evaluation

Figure 3.4 represents the four types of people that organizations are comprised of.

- In the lower left quadrant are those people whose performance is unacceptable and who will never fit into the Lean culture that is being created. These people should not be a part of the organization.

- In the upper right quadrant are the high potential people—the people the company can be built upon. However, where does H.R. tend to spend the most time? Most organizations spend most of their time dealing with the problem people in the lower left quadrant when they should be spending time developing high potential people. If we do not spend time developing our good people, they will leave. They will become disenchanted and find more rewarding work elsewhere.

- In the upper left quadrant are those people who have the heart and desire to fit into the Lean culture but whose performance is still unacceptable. Work with these people. They may be in the wrong job, lack training, are uninspired, and so on. Help them move into the upper right quadrant. We want all of our people to be in the upper right quadrant. We want people who fit into the new Lean culture and are achieving the results necessary to support the business objectives of the organization.

- In the lower right quadrant is the person (as described earlier) who is getting acceptable performance using fear, intimidation, and a command and control style of management in his or her work group. The question becomes—can they adopt the habits of the new culture and leave the old habits behind? Again, the goal is for everyone to be in the upper right quadrant.

Most organizations have difficulty dealing with the people in the lower right quadrant. Often, these individuals have been with the organization 10-20 years and were advanced and promoted when they "got things done" using a command and control style of management. They received good-to-excellent performance reviews year after year. The organization essentially created and promoted this managerial or supervisory style and now feels guilty because these people resist adopting a Lean Culture. Adopting a Lean Culture is extremely difficult for these individuals because their management style and behaviors have become a deeply ingrained set of habits. Unfortunately, not dealing with these individuals can have the following consequences:

- If these individuals have enough people reporting to them, they can literally stop the Lean implementation. An organizational restart of Lean after that point may not be successful.

- If the organization's "guilt" causes such individuals to be given "more leash" or to be treated differently, resentment toward management may build. It also sends the signal that an individual does not have be a supporter of Lean to survive in the organization.

- Not dealing with this situation will diminish the organization's initial excitement for Lean when the organization begins to understand that needed changes to improve the organization will not be made.

Dealing with these individuals should always be direct, and actions can take a couple of different routes. Note that all actions regarding individuals must be done in a manner that maintains an individual's dignity and respect while following all state and federal legal guidelines. Suggested routes include the following:

- Moving the individual to a "Special Projects" position in which the individual does productive work but has no one reporting to him or her. This action usually applies to high seniority individuals.
- Put the individual on the 90-day plan. Experience has shown that, if individuals will not make significant changes in 90 days, a longer period will not matter.

The 90-day plan has the following components which should be well documented:

1) Start with this one-on-one discussion between the leader and the individual: The company is taking a bus ride to become a World Class organization. This journey is necessary for the company to survive in the future. The company wants you on this bus; you know our people, processes, and customers. Because we will be operating in a Lean environment with a Lean Culture, we are changing how the organization is led and managed. To obtain a ticket for this bus ride, here are the specific behaviors you must leave behind and here are the specific behaviors you must adopt (refer to the organization's behavioral expectations if possible). What do you need from the company to help you accomplish these changes? The consequences of not obtaining a bus ticket should also be discussed.

2) Once the above discussion is completed, the new expectations are clear, and a plan of help is established, then weekly or bi-weekly review and update sessions are set up. These sessions allow both the company and the individual to discuss whether progress is being made.

   Note that the leader's discussion of progress or a lack of must be based on "firsthand, observable information," as discussed on page 100—Focus on Behavior. The leader must make almost daily observations in meetings, on the job site, and so forth, and note these observations in a notebook to be shared with the individual at their next weekly/bi-weekly meeting. All sessions should end with the question—what do you need from the company to help you accomplish these changes?

3) By the 60-day mark, a trend should be clear and a forecast made (assuming nothing changes) to the individual of where he or she will be at 90 days. Again, all sessions should end with the question—what do you need from the company to help you accomplish these changes?

4) At 90 days, the successful individual is congratulated and his or her performance is now assessed under the regular performance review system, which has been upgraded to include Lean and Lean Culture.

The unsuccessful individual should be connected to an outplacement service. Remember, the individual's dignity and respect must be maintained throughout this entire process.

The owner of a custom manufacturer decided he wanted to implement Lean. It was clear from the beginning of the training and implementation that the organization's lead foreman, with 15 years of seniority, saw no need to do anything different. The hourly associates, though, were excited about the changes that Lean represented and were very involved in making improvements. In spite of the lack of participation of the lead foreman, the organization made a 20% productivity improvement in the first year. This improvement resulted in reduced lead times, improved deliveries, and an improved bottom-line.

Although the owner was very happy with the results, we approached him and told him that further progress would be limited by this foreman and that he might reverse the changes after our planned exit. We suggested that he be talked to and the "bus ride" World Class journey scenario explained. The owner's response was "oh, he'll be okay—he just needs more training!"

The additional training made no difference. There was no bus ride discussion. Six months later, when an opening developed for the organization's plant superintendent position, he was promoted (without our involvement). Convinced that nothing had really changed, the hourly associates gave up. The new superintendent allowed all the improvements made in the first year to eventually go back to the way they were.

Ultimately, the owner decided that loyalty trumped accountability and organizational performance, which we guess in this case was okay. It was his money.

On page 112 in the book *Leading Change*, noted organizational change expert John Kotter addresses this type of employee and provides additional supporting strategies for handling this situation.

Additional H.R. Lean responsibilities include monitoring and testing for the completeness of the communication and empowerment plan. Measuring communication effectiveness means testing it using activities such as the following:

- Management By Walking Around (MBWA)—randomly asking associates what, when, how, and why questions about strategies and goals that have been communicated.
- Monitoring the amount of rumors in the organization. Rumors have only one reason to exist in an organization—to fill in gaps in communication.
- The types of questions during the Q & A session at the required monthly "all-hands" company meetings—are people asking questions they should already know the answers to?
- Are all business areas visually communicating with the rest of the company? Can a person tell what is going on in the organization from the visual communication?

Part of the evaluation of the completeness of both the communication and empowerment plan should rely on the use of surveys performed by outside companies.

Lean Culture Case Study – Wiremold

The Wiremold Company is often used as an example of how Lean can be used to successfully improve (turnaround) an American company. While Wiremold is a manufacturer of office wire and cable management solutions, its classic use of Lean to improve the organization, as we will show, applies to construction, healthcare, or service.

The following figure shows the status of the company in 1990-91:

Wiremold's Status in 1990-1991

- Low Profits
- No Cash
- No Growth
- Bad Customer Service
- Losing Market Share

The family owners of Wiremold, worried that the company was about to go out of business, hired a new CEO, Art Byrne. Art and the Lean executives he assembled at Wiremold started to make changes. They knew that Lean was continuous improvement through waste elimination, but they also understood that the organization's culture had to change. Initially, Art used his own behaviors as the model and example for his senior managers to adopt. Using Toyota's "respect for people" emphasis, Wiremold ultimately created the organizational Code of Conduct shown on page 60. It was Wiremold's one-page H.R. manual. Associates could be terminated based on repeated violations of the Code.

As noted, to reinforce the code at Wiremold, the Leadership Team members would circulate among the workforce on a regular basis, asking team members to "tell me one part of the code."

Wiremold initially focused the use of the Lean Tools on eliminating waste related to its immediate company needs and goals—cash and customer service. In fact, the first Kaizen that Art facilitated was an order entry process. The following Lean Tools were focused on:

- 5c's (5S)
- Visual Management
- One piece flow lines
- Machine Setup Reduction
- Kanbans

At the same time, they set up measurements that would help them measure the achievement of their organizational goals:

- Customer Service
- Productivity
- Inventory/working capital turns
- Reduction in defects (quality)
- 5c's and degree of visual management
- Profit sharing

By 1999, Wiremold had achieved the following results:

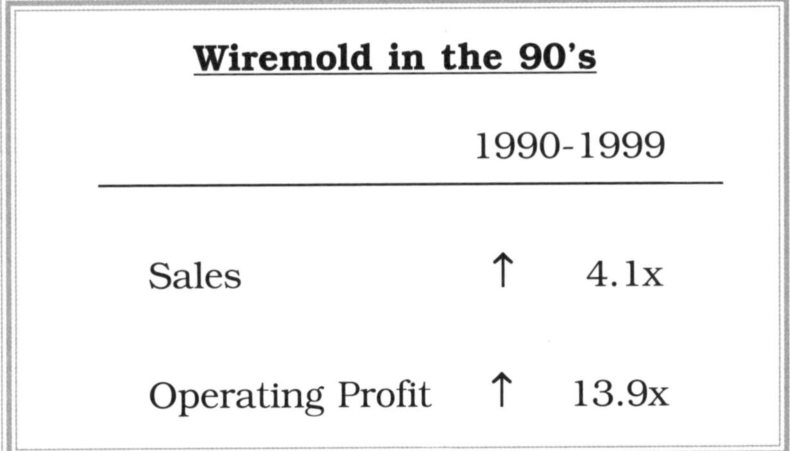

Wiremold in the 90's

	1990-1999	
Sales	↑	4.1x
Operating Profit	↑	13.9x

In 2000, the Wiremold organization was sought out and purchased by a company for $505.07 per share. This share value represented a 1,861% increase from 1990.

Wiremold did many things right and achieved outstanding results while, in their own words, "just scratching the surface." Their story provides an outline that would serve most companies well.

Unfortunately, the company that bought Wiremold did not know about Lean and was not interested in learning about it. Art Byrne retired in 2002, and by 2006, the new owners had demolished Lean. The layoffs started shortly after that.

Lean can only be successfully implemented from the top—and it can be destroyed from there also.

Chapter Summary

Organizational culture is a learned process and is developed by the organization as a response to the working environment established by the organization's leadership and management team.

American businesses spend little or no time developing and establishing a Lean culture or any other culture in their organizations. Unfortunately, a culture develops in every organization whether it is directed and guided or not. Left unguided, it usually develops at the supervisory level, and this culture, in most cases, is not the culture the organization would knowingly choose.

Behavioral expectations can be the start of your organization's guided Lean Culture development process. The H.R. area is then responsible for closing the feedback loop on the people side between "the strategy, culture, and plan we say we are deploying" and the actual deployment.

References

AMI (Producer). (1999) *Joel Barker's Leadershift [DVD]*

Emiliani, B. (2007) *Better Thinking, Better Results* (2nd ed.). Kensington, CT: The Center for Lean Business Management, LLC.

Fayad, V. and Rubrich, L. (2009) *Policy Deployment and Lean Implementation Planning* (Rev. ed.). Fort Wayne, IN: WCM Associates LLC.

Haviland, W.A. (1987) *Cultural Anthropology* (5th ed.) New York, NY: Holt, Rinehart and Winston.

Koenigsaecker, G. (2009) *Leading the Lean Enterprise Transformation.* New York, NY: Productivity Press.

Kotter, J. (1996) *Leading Change.* Boston, MA: Harvard Business Review Press.

Mann, David. (2005) *Creating a Lean Culture.* New York: Productivity Press.

Ryan, D. "The Wiremold Story." Powerpoint Presentation.

Spreitzer, G. and Quinn, R. (2001) *A Company of Leaders.* San Francisco, CA: Jossey-Bass.

Chapter 4

The Core Lean Tools

- 5Ss
- Teams
- Standard Work
- Value Stream Maps
- A3 Problem Solving
- Error Proofing
- Office Cells
- Kanbans

For Shops:

- Setup Reduction
- Total Productive Maintenance (TPM)

> **"World Class facilities develop beginning with the 5Ss, and facilities that fail, fall apart beginning with the 5Ss."**
>
> HIROYUKI HIRANO
> 5 PILLARS OF THE VISUAL WORKPLACE

This chapter identifies, defines, and gives examples of the Core Lean Tools that are used in all industries to eliminate the waste that is common to all. Each tool is designed to target a particular type of business waste:

- 5S – Improves safety and eliminates searching, looking, or hunting for anything (including computer files)
- Teams – Provide a format for problems to be solved and waste to be eliminated using the best ideas available at that time
- Standard Work – Reduces scrap, rework, and reconciliations
- Value Stream Maps – Help identify business waste, are extremely effective at reducing information and physical product lead times
- A3 Problem Solving – Structured team-based problem solving
- Error Proofing – Prevents human errors from turning into defects. The only Lean Tool that can be used to develop perfect information product or physical product quality
- Office Cells – Reduce information product lead time, reduce scrap and rework
- Kanbans – Reduce inventory while reducing or eliminating material outages or shortages
- Setup Reduction – Improves the shop's manufacturing capacity, reduces scrap, reduces shop lead time

- Total Productive Maintenance (TPM) – Improves the shop's manufacturing uptime, reduces scrap, reduces shop lead time

Again, the waste that is targeted for elimination is the waste that is preventing us from achieving our business goals as identified in Policy Deployment. For many organizations, the lack of consistent execution of basic business fundamentals (as noted in Chapter 2) on a shift-by-shift, and day-by-day basis makes it one of the initial goals. This goal requires starting with the 5S and Standard Work tools.

5S

The 5Ss are about creating a safe, clean, and organized business environment. They attack organizational waste related to the following:

- Injury or lost time accidents due to unsafe work conditions (there is no 6th S for safety).

- Searching, hunting, or looking for anything—at the jobsite, office, shop, service trucks, computer, or anywhere!

Because having a safe, clean, and organized business is the foundation of becoming a World Class organization, 5S is usually the first tool deployed by most organizations. Implementing the 5Ss is often accomplished by the Leadership Team in their own areas first as an enabler activity in Step 7 of PD (Develop Lean Implementation Plan).

The other advantage to implementing 5S first is that, with the discipline necessary to be successful with 5S in place, the rest of the Lean tools are easier to implement.

Why 5S?

A Buffalo, New York, countertop installation contractor had very disorganized trucks. Workers were always looking for tools or materials. It often took at least 15 to 30 minutes for them find the tools or materials and get back to work. Sometimes the tools or materials they were looking for were not even in the truck or on the jobsite. By the time they realized a tool was missing, sometimes it was too late to back track.

Each truck was 5S'd, and they were made identical. Workers did not have to search for tools or inventory. Missing tools were quickly identified and traced back to their last known location. This company grew from $700K to $12M in 12 years.

The 5Ss, in implementation order, are as follows:

Sort – Decide what is needed and what is not needed in the work area. The general criterion is, if an item in the work area has not been used in the last 30 days and will not be used in the next 30 days, then you need to move it out of the work area. Items are moved out of the work area using the "5S red tag" system.

- 5S red tags are the way we identify items we want to move out of our work area. Once tagged, these items are moved to the "red tag parking lot." The red tag parking lot is a clear storage space in the office or shop. An individual or team is then assigned to go through the parking lot and designate the status of the items. This status can include restore in a different location, send back to supplier, or throw away.

Straighten/Set in Order – Establish a place for everything and put everything in its place. Mark and label locations using company-developed standards. A straightened work area means that anyone from outside that work area should be able to find something in 30 seconds or less.

Sweep/Shine – Sweep and shine the area completely using a top-down approach. Clean and paint as required to make things look like new. Design ways to contain or prevent messes to keep future cleanups small.

Schedule/Standardize – Standardize and maintain the use of sort, straighten, and sweep. Use a 5S checklist by area—checklists are 5S job instructions—to ensure uniformity and eliminate variation.

Sustain – Sustain the gains from the first four steps. This is the difficult part as noted in Chapter 2. In this step, an audit process is established (until the 5Ss become part of the organization's culture) not only to ensure that the gains are maintained but also to make recommendations on how to continuously improve the area.

5S also applies to the jobsite with the goal of eliminating searching and hunting. Obviously, Straighten/Set in Order is a real challenge for the jobsite because, ideally, everything is flowing and changing.

A typical practice at a jobsite is to clean up on a weekly basis, usually Fridays. Because 5S is about eliminating the waste of searching for materials that reduces "tool time," consideration must be given to cleaning and organizing on a daily basis. The thinking is that cleaning and organizing on a daily basis "nets out" overall to create a safer jobsite with more tool time than cleaning once per week does.

Figure 4.1
Construction Tool Crib Before 5S
(Courtesy Grunau Company)

Figure 4.2
Construction Tool Crib After 5S
(Courtesy Grunau Company)

A few other thoughts on 5S:

- Demonstrating organizational leadership means the Leadership Team, managers, and supervisors would never "just walk by" an unsafe or dirty work environment. This leadership helps develop a Lean Culture in which no one in the organization would knowingly walk by an unsafe or dirty work condition.

- The 5S red tagging event is a "one-time" activity, not an annual activity that allows us to make excuses for what our area looks like during the year. If everyone is properly trained in 5S, they will protect "their area" from things that do not belong there and move things to the "5S parking lot" when they are no longer needed.

- Organizations generally require their shop and trade associates to clean up their areas during or at the end of their shifts. However, in the same organization, a third party is brought in to clean up the offices of the administrative associates. If we want teamwork, we need one set of rules.

- When 5S fails, it fails because we did not properly implement the 4th S (Schedule/Standardize) and there was no follow-up using the 5th S (Sustain).

- One of the required measures for the success of a 5S implementation includes never having to clean up in advance of visits from owners or other special company visitors. Think about it—when we tell our associates they must "clean up" before a visitor arrives, what are we telling them?

This tool applies in all businesses and in every area. Again, 5S is the foundation for all the other tools. If you cannot maintain a safe, clean, and organized work environment, you can never be a World Class organization.

Teams

In Chapter 3, the importance of using teams in a Lean implementation and how to create an environment in which teamwork can develop were discussed. This section discusses the use of teams in Policy Deployment project implementations using Kaizen Events.

Kaizen is a Japanese word that means to "change for the good"—doing little things better every day—continuous improvement (CI). The target of Kaizen is cost reduction through the elimination of waste at all levels of the process. Kaizen has become part of the Japanese culture in manufacturing, especially at organizations like Toyota.

Unfortunately, Americans have trouble thinking in terms of slow and continuous improvement. Americans want giant steps, dramatic improvement, and homeruns, so there is a difference between how the Japanese and Americans use Kaizen. For U.S. Companies, a Kaizen Event includes the following:

- A team of people (5-12)
    - Associates from the work site.
    - Associates and management people who interface with the work site.

- Outside eyes (hourly or salaried). These individuals should be unfamiliar with the process and should not be afraid to ask questions and challenge current thinking.

- Spending three to ten days (as required) focused on an organizational process to accomplish a particular PD goal.
- The intent is to cause rapid, dramatic performance improvement in the process.
- Event timing is based on the *Accountable* and *Responsible* team's commitment in PD Step 7.

Prior to the event, the organization's Certified Lean Facilitator collects data and prepares for the event. A Kaizen Event starts with the Lean Facilitator training the team on one of the Lean Tools to ensure common understanding and concludes when the team has accomplished the initial goal. Near the end of the Kaizen Event, the team elects a team leader.

The 15 steps of a Kaizen Event

Step #0—Event Preparation - Select event area and team and create team package.

1. Area selection based on Policy Deployment.
2. Team selection – see above.
3. Team package is the written documentation used as background and reference information during the event:
   - Definition of the problem
   - Owner's requirements
   - Processing at each operation
   - How to handle abnormal conditions

- Event budget and how to obtain supplies
- Event support personnel contact list
- Results of prior events or improvements

Step #1—Define the scope and goals of the event.

1. Goals are defined based on the reasons the event area was chosen.
2. Write goals on a flip chart.

Step #2—Train the team. Review the Lean Construction Tool(s) and techniques that support the team's goal.

1. Training on the focus of the event—Value Stream Mapping (VSM), 5S, Kanban, TPM, Setup Reduction, Construction tools, and so on.
2. Include stages of team development.

Step #3—Walk the event area, observe physical layout, review videos if available. This step starts the idea creation process.

1. Allows everyone on the team to see the current situation and potentially dispel any misconceptions they have about the process.
2. Review goals of the event during the walk through.

Step #4—Collect data on event area (scrap, production, time studies, videos, etc.). Develop/obtain the baseline performance measurements.

Collect data on the event area required by the team. Examples:

1. Number of associates
2. Amount of inventory
3. Size of area

4. Other pertinent information

Step #5—Brainstorm ideas—Thinking "outside the box" and piggybacking are important here.

Follow the brainstorming rules shown on page 64-65.

Step #6—Use multi-voting to prioritize the top 8 to 10 ideas that will be worked on immediately.

Conduct a "reality check" to confirm that implementing the top 8 to 10 ideas will achieve the goal.

Step #7—Form sub-teams to go out and implement ideas.

Team members are assigned to or volunteer for specific ideas.

Step #8—Check results. Each sub-team reviews their results with the entire team so that consensus can be developed on the direction of each sub-team.

Consider

1. Simulating process
2. Taking time observations
3. Video recording process

Step #9—Develop/Review/Update all operator instructions for all successful ideas.

1. Provide time for the team to train associates in new procedures.
2. Make sure updates are formally documented.

Step #10—Develop an Action Plan for all unimplemented ideas using a Kaizen Newspaper (Figure 4.3). The Kaizen Newspaper plan must include what will be done, who will do it, and when it will be accomplished.

The event area must be fully process ready, all Standard Work must be updated and posted, and all associates must be trained in the new sequence or methods before the team leaves the area.

Step #11—Report Out to management on the results of the event. During the afternoon of the last event day, the team will give management a verbal "Report Out" of the activities accomplished and the action plan.

Basic "report out" format:

- Restate the original goals
- Provide "before" documentation
- Provide "after" documentation
- Show videos or pictures of the event
- Review the Action Plan for incomplete improvement ideas

Step #12—Recognize the team.

Step #13—"After Event" follow-up by team on all Open Action Items.

Step #14—Measure event area improvements.

Step #15—Team disbands when all Open Action Items are completed.

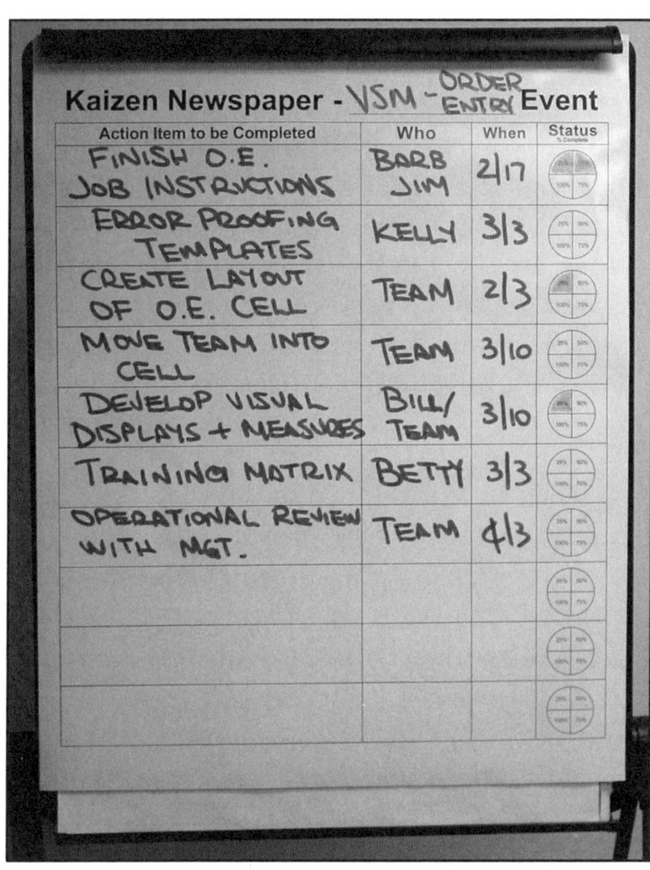

Figure 4.3
Kaizen Event Newspaper

Kaizen Events are a powerful improvement activity! Unfortunately, Kaizen Events are often misused. They have become an "end all" to themselves. Organizations do Kaizen Events just to do them or schedule a certain number of events to be completed on a regular basis. These events are often called random, point, or drive-by Kaizen Events. Again, when examined, organizations are found to have hundreds of wasteful activities that cannot all be eliminated at once. Use Kaizen Events to focus only on the projects and improvements that support the organization's goals deployed throughout the company in Policy Deployment.

Kaizen Events are often misused!

Standard Work

In general, American businesses lack the discipline to consistently write or follow process procedures throughout their organization (including all shifts). Even our well-written ISO registration procedures are collecting dust on the shelf. The result is lower quality, reduced productivity, variation, and Kaizen Events in which the results are not sustained. These are the outcomes when the discipline of Standard Work does not exist.

Standard Work is a difficult concept for the Construction Industry because every project is generally a one-off and all the processes inside the project are broad-brushed with this thinking. However, there are certain processes inside the project that repeat:

- Estimating
- Purchasing
- Pre-fabrication
- Sub-contractor shop manufacturing such as HVAC ducting
- Project Management
- Project budget formats
- Project reporting
- Project communications
- Lean Project Scheduling
- Drywall hanging
- And many more

Standard Work is defined as the documented procedures and methods for people and machines (or office equipment) to work together to perform value added work while minimizing all forms of process waste.

Standard Work

- Documents the *safest*, *best*, and *easiest* way to do a job (the *fastest* will be an outcome of this).
- Focuses on the process procedure (not the person or the outcome).
- Establishes a pattern/routine/habit for the process to be accomplished.
- Establishes a baseline for improvement.
- Makes staffing and scheduling a process or procedure easier.
- Is a living document that changes as improvements are made.

Standard Work means that associates

- Follow the same documented procedures each time.
- Do the same sequence of work each time.
- Use the same tools, supplies, machines, and equipment each time.
- Store supplies and raw materials in the same place every day.

Standard Work then also applies to pre-fabrication areas. Although the pre-fabricated product changes for each project, creating Standard Work at the beginning of the project ensures the highest quality and productivity for the life of each pre-fabricated product.

Standard Work is a part of Daily Management. Daily Management is the "basic execution" of business fundamentals in an organization required to serve owner/customers and be profitable on a day-to-day basis. A

World Class organization can be built only on a strong foundation of a workforce and processes that are under control. Lean and Lean improvements require the discipline of having procedures in place throughout the organization that all associates follow. Lean can be successful only when the daily business fundamentals are under control—those things done on a daily basis to serve the owner/customers and run the business.

Without the discipline of Daily Management and the updating of improvements with new Standard Work, Lean or any other type of improvements are not sustainable. See the following figures.

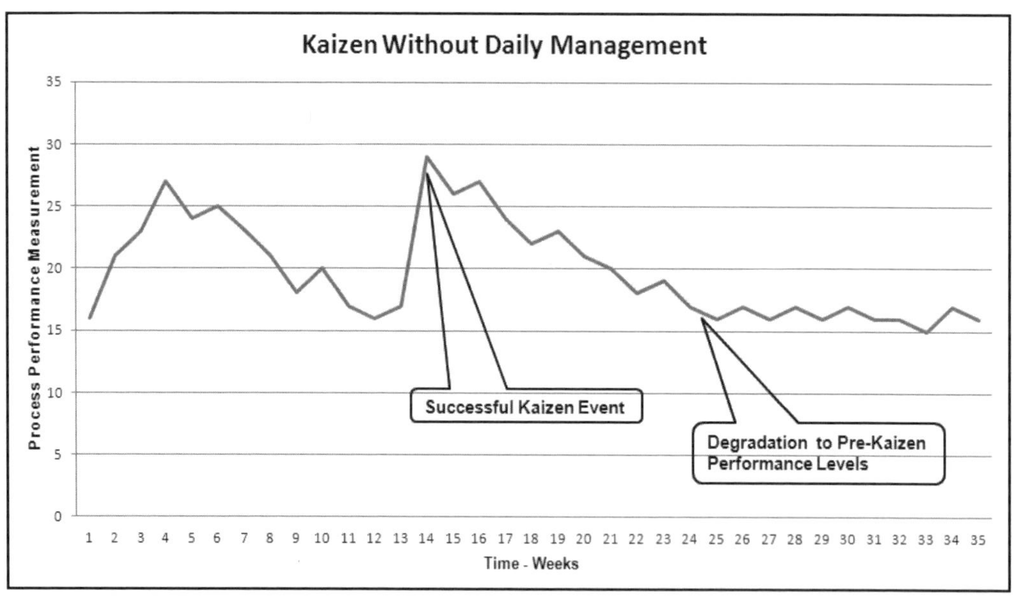

Figure 4.4

Without the discipline of Daily Management in place, the successful Kaizen Event of week 14 (shown in Figure 4.4) degrades until, at week 25, the process is performing at pre-Kaizen levels. At that point, the cost of the Kaizen Event can be added to the organization's list of waste.

There are two primary reasons for this degradation occurring:

1) No Standard Work = no process improvement update, so over time, the process goes back to the way it was because that is what everyone remembers and is comfortable with.
2) The Kaizen Event was completed with "outside the process area resources." There is no buy-in from the process operators who did not participate (or had limited involvement) in the improvement. When everyone leaves, the process begins to revert almost immediately even if there was a Standard Work update.

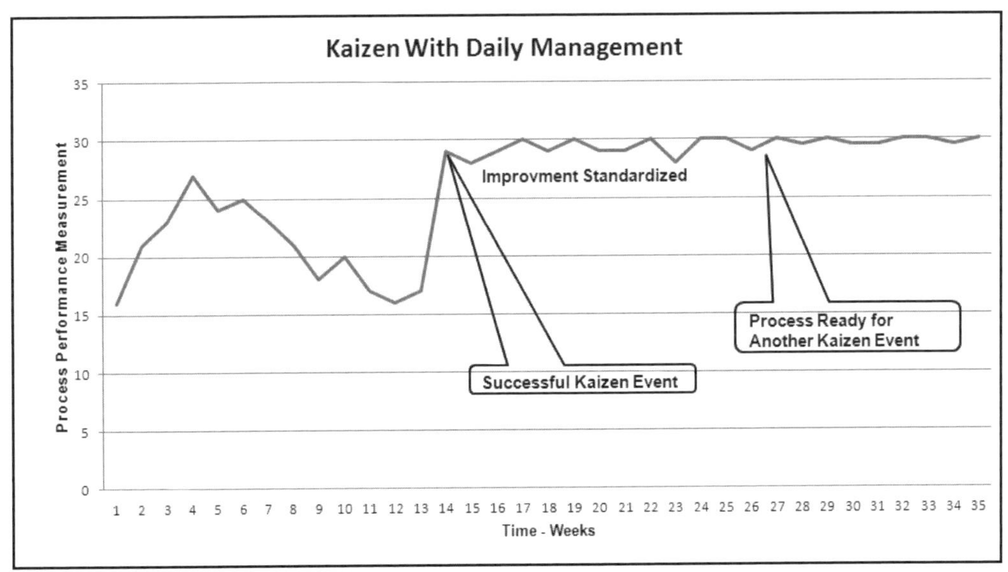

Figure 4.5

Figure 4.5 shows the results of another successful Kaizen Event. At the end of this event, the process operators who were involved in the event create or update the Standard Work themselves. Standard daily visual process measurements are created. All remaining process operators are trained in the new Standard Work. The improvement is standardized and stabilizes over time. This process is then ready for another Kaizen Event (assuming it is one of the Kaizen Events established in Policy Deployment).

Standard Work, also called Standard Operations, includes the following:

- Takt Time
- Standard Work Distribution and Sequence
- Standard Work Sheets

Takt Time

Takt is a German word that means "time beat" or rhythm. Takt Time (TT) is the rate at which a sub's shop or a pre-fabrication area must supply the project to keep the flow of work moving or the rate at which the trade partners must clear a room or floor to keep the project on schedule. Producing at a rate faster than TT will build inventory while producing at a rate slower than TT will shut this area of the jobsite down or produce trade partner delays.

Note that TT is different from "cycle time." Cycle time is the length of time it takes to complete one step in a process. If the room completion process has four different steps, for example, framing, electrical, plumbing, and drywall, there would be four different cycle times.

Takt time (TT) is the available shop, pre-fabrication, or trade partner processing time divided by the total of the jobsite's requirements for a part or assembly.

Takt Time is calculated as follows:

$$\textbf{Takt Time} = \frac{\textbf{Total Daily Processing Time}}{\textbf{Total Daily Jobsite Requirements}}$$

Processing time does not include breaks, lunches (unrelieved breaks and lunches), 5S time, meeting time, or any time not available to process the jobsite's needs.

Standard Work Distribution and Sequence

Standard work distribution and sequence documents in a diagram how each team member performs a series of repetitive steps within a process. It may be different from the actual process steps (additional value added activities may be added to eliminate waiting time). It compares the cycle time of each step of the process to the TT to make sure the TT is not exceeded.

Standard Work Sheet

A Standard Work Sheet is created when all the cycle times are below the TT. It documents safety, quality, Work-In-Process, cycle time, and sequence of steps. It also displays team member movements, if required by the process. (Figure 4.6)

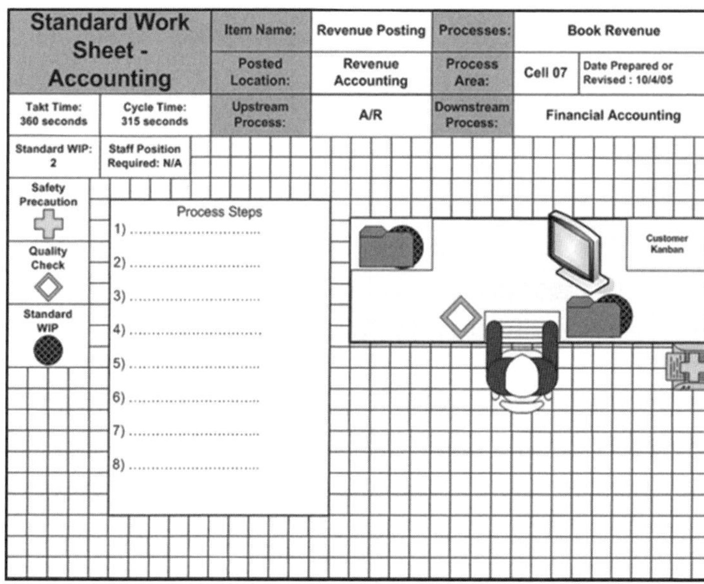

Figure 4.6
Standard Work Sheet

When the process step instructions (job instructions) are long, they may be included on separate sheets as shown below.

Figure 4.7
Job Instructions (Courtesy of Grunau Company)

Remember that, because written instructions are subject to interpretation, you should maximize the use of pictures when creating job instructions.

Standard Work is a "living document" that represents the safest, easiest, and best process/steps/methods known today. Following Standard Work improves productivity while reducing errors and variation, thereby improving quality. Standard Work allows us to design processes that will meet the customer's delivery requirements.

As "waste" is identified in the current process, improvements are made, and the Standard Work is updated to standardize the improvement.

Value Stream Maps

Value Stream Mapping (VSM) is the only Core Lean Tool that will not eliminate waste. Its sole purpose is to help organizations identify the waste that is preventing them from reaching their organizational goals. Once the waste is identified, the appropriate waste elimination Lean tool can be pulled from the gangbox and deployed to eliminate the waste.

Value Stream Mapping creates a one-page picture of a process (although it may be the length of a wall page—see Figure 4.8), identifying all the steps, sequences, touches, delays, and cycle times for each step of the process. Many organizations start by mapping the "system cycle time"—from the time a customer requests a product or service to the time the customer receives a completed product or service (the RFP process, for example). VSM is most effective in identifying how to improve system efficiency.

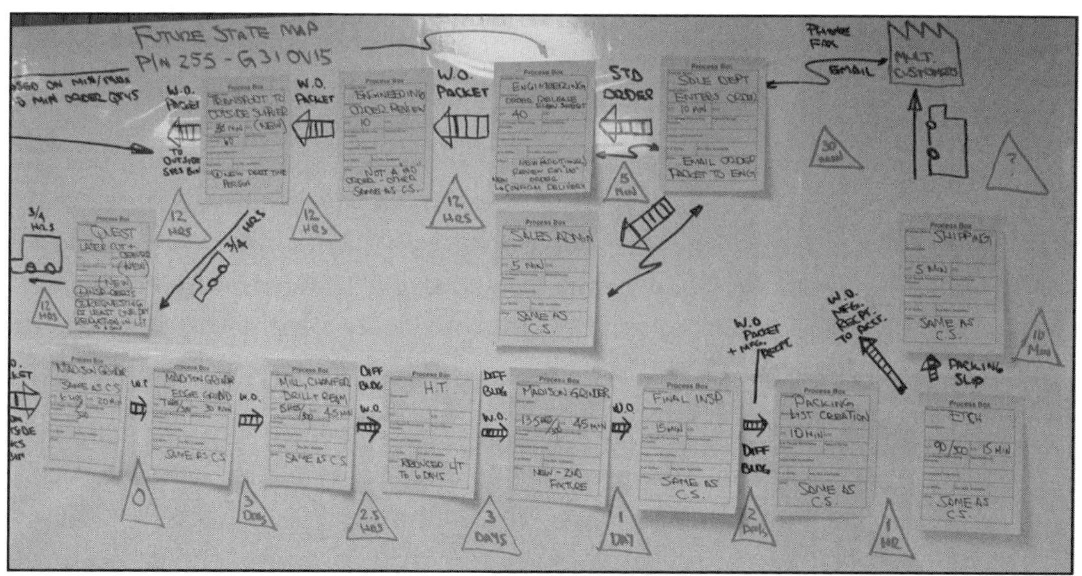

Figure 4.8
Value Stream Map

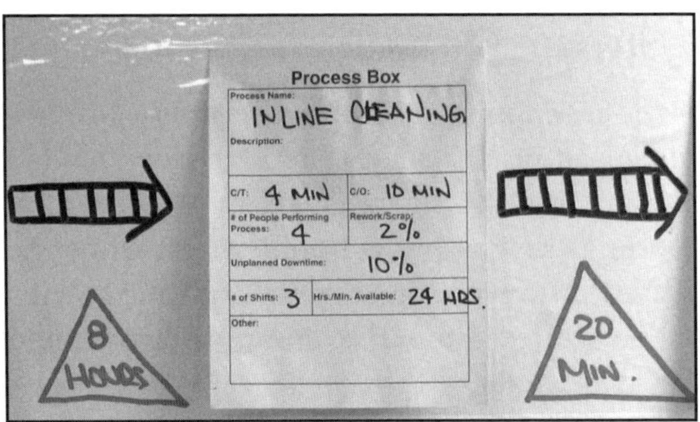

Figure 4.9
VSM Component—Process Box

A major icon/element of a VSM, shown in Figure 4.9, is a process box. A process box is an operation, step, or touch in the VSM. It may be a value added or a non-value added step. It has locations on the form to record the cycle time, number of people performing the step, yield to account for scrap, changeover/setup time (if any), operation downtime, number of shifts the step runs, and the total hours the step is staffed. The black arrows before and after the step indicate that this is "push" production (versus pull). The triangles represent process or inventory delays. In Figure 4.9, there are 8 hours of inventory upstream of the cleaning operation. Any new work that is moved to "cleaning" from the previous step will suffer, on average, an 8 hour delay before it is started. Downstream from cleaning, there is a 20 minute delay before the next operation is started.

Delays in construction represented by the triangles can occur in many places throughout the entire delivery system, including the following:

- Waiting for owner decisions

- Purchasing delays because people are working on other projects
- Project manager decision delays
- Searching and hunting
- Incomplete or wrong data
- Space or sequence conflicts with other trades
- Lost, missing, or undelivered material
- RFIs
- And many others

It should be noted that VSM is the most misused of all the Lean tools. Often, maps are created with no specific organizational goal or improvement in mind other than to map a process. As we noted earlier, most organizations have hundreds of problems that can be revealed by the map, so where do you start? It is recommended that the following four-step VSM process and guidelines be used:

Step 1

Pick the process, service, project, or administrative process to map (improve). An improvement goal(s) is required. Again, this goal should tie into the organizational goals.

Criteria for Goal Selection:

- From Policy Deployment
- A new or changed business goal, owner requirement, or business condition. (VSM's are best at lead time reductions.)

Anything other than these criteria qualifies as random and should not be mapped! (Policy Deployment requires no other Lean activities.)

Remember, all goals must be **SMART** goals! **S**pecific, **M**easurable, **A**chievable, **R**elevant, and **T**ime dimensioned.

Step 2

Create the "Current State" VSM (CSVSM).

Do not forget about the office/information product leadtime. Often delays, waiting, and other waste in the office are left off of the maps of a shop or jobsite VSM.

- Identify all potential improvements (Kaizen Events) via "star burst" sticky notes and brainstorming.

- Normal brainstorming activity:

    - Brainstorm following rules
    - Affinitize similar ideas
    - Secret ballot vote for best ideas
    - Go as far down on the "voted for" list as the group thinks is necessary

- Focus/prioritize on "low cost" or "no cost" improvements that support Step 1's goal(s).

- Verify management support.

Step 3

Create the "Future State" VSM (FSVSM).

- The "Future State" VSM must meet the goal(s) established in Step 1. Forcing the FSVSM to meet the goal generally requires "outside the box thinking."

- If the initial FSVSM does not meet the goal(s) established in Step 1, go further down the brainstorming "voted for" list or brainstorm again.

Step 4

Develop an Action Plan (Kaizen Newspaper, Figure 4.3, page 141) to make the FSVSM the new CSVSM.

- The responsibility for completing the Action Plan is always the VSM team's. This responsibility is never handed-off.
- The accountable person from the VSM Event team (the buck stops here) is the "Who" on the Kaizen Newspaper. This person can recruit other non-VSM Event associates to help do the implementation but he/she remains responsible.
- The "When" date is always determined by the "Who" (accountable person) so we can hold them responsible. If it is a safety related issue, it is not given a date or time but must be completed immediately.
- The team disbands, with celebration, when all open Action Items are completed.

VSM General Guidelines

Use a VSM Checklist to help you prepare for the event (if you don't have one, send an e-mail to info@wcmfg.com and we will send you one). From our checklist, here are some items of particular importance:

- Determine resources needed to support customers during the event. The VSM Event must be transparent to your customers.

- Communicate with the entire facility about the upcoming event. Make sure that everyone knows.

- Communicate with the jobsite/office/shop/process supervisor(s) (and others who will be affected) about the event and its objectives. This is a face-to-face meeting, not a memo, an e-mail, or a voice mail.

- Advise the team members who work in the project area/process about the upcoming event—again, this communication should be face-to-face. (Note—let these people know that their input along with their fellow workers' input is crucial while the team is evaluating and changing its process.)

- Arrange lunches for each training day. Invite process decision makers/managers to lunch each day as a way of reviewing VSM direction, ideas, and progress. Doing so prevents any surprise management concerns or objections at the "Event Report Out." (This activity applies to Kaizen Events also.)

- Determine who will be invited to the Event Report Out on the last day of the event. On day one of the event, notify these individuals of the date, time, and location of the Report Out. However, you may make minor adjustments in the actual starting time on the day before or morning of the Report Out.

By creating Value Stream Maps, an organization begins to "see" the waste in the organization and can systematically attack the waste based on the PD goals.

A3 Team Problem Solving

Like all the tools in the "Core Lean Tool Box," A3 Team Problem Solving is a very powerful tool, from both a Lean Culture development standpoint and as a structured/standard work problem solver. Unfortunately, many organizations jump to Toyota's A3 Problem Solving as a "magic pill" or "silver bullet" to unravel their seeming lack of problem-solving skills without understanding that it is their lack of a supporting Lean Culture that prevents them from effectively using *any* problem-solving technique.

A3 refers to a European paper size that is roughly equivalent to an American 11"x17" tabloid size paper. The requirement to use a single sheet forces the team to report their information in a clear, concise manner.

The A3 format is used by Toyota as the template for three different types of A3 reports:

- Proposals
- Status
- Problem Solving

In the United States, the A3 format is used for many different report types. For example, in Target Value Design (TVD), A3s are used to document areas of cost reduction evaluated to eliminate the waste of redundant evaluations.

There is no "magic" in the steps that the structured A3 Problem Solving template takes a team through. These steps follow the Deming PDCA cycle. with Steps 1 through 5 being the "Plan," Step 6 being the "Do," Step 7 being the "Check," and Step 8 being the "Act."

The steps are:

1. Identify the Problem or Need
2. Understand the Current Situation/State
3. Develop the Goal Statement—Develop the Target State
4. Perform Root Cause Analysis
5. Brainstorm/Determine Countermeasures
6. Create Countermeasures Implementation Plan
7. Check Results—Confirmation of Effect
8. Update Standard Work

On the A3 template, the steps are typically laid out as shown in figure 4.10:

A3 Problem Solving
Problem Solving Tools on Back Side

Process: ______
Originator: ______ Date: ______

1) Identify the Problem or Need

2) Understanding the Current Situation/State

3) Goal Statement – Develop the Target State (must meet the business goals deployed in Policy Deployment)

4) Root Cause Analysis (see also back side of this form)

5) Brainstorm/Determine Countermeasures

6) Countermeasures Implementation Plan

Action Item to be Completed	Who	When	Status

7) Check Results – Confirmation of Effect

8) Update Standard Work

What	Accountable	When

Figure 4.10
A3 Problem Solving Template

If you would like a complimentary copy of an A3 template, please e-mail us at info@wcmfg.com.

Surprisingly, these steps and format look very much like templates created by U.S. companies in the '80s and '90s. Ford Motor Company created an 8 1/2" x 11" Problem Solving template called an "8D." Johnson Controls, Inc., created a Problem Solving Document (PSD) using both sides of a form that folds to an 8 1/2" x 11" size, but is larger than tabloid size unfolded. If U.S. companies had the structured templates and knowledge of the problem-solving tools, why aren't U.S. organizations better problem solvers?

The answer is Lean Culture. When most organizations start their Lean implementation, they jump to using the Lean Tools. As we noted in Chapter 2, there are four components of a Lean implementation: Lean Planning, Lean Concepts, Lean Tools, and Lean Culture. The Lean Tools are ineffective without the support of a developing Lean Culture. This supporting Lean Culture is illustrated by how Toyota views problems:

- Problems are seen as opportunities to improve their processes and ultimately their products.
- The people assigned to solving the problem view the assignment as an opportunity to improve their problem-solving skills. They understand that they learn more and become better problem solvers each time they perform the process.

In Toyota, no problem is a problem!

Compare this attitude to how a typical U.S. company associate views problem solving. We view it as a "burden" or maybe even a punishment to be given the responsibility to solve a problem. We get through it so we can check it off our to-do list.

A3 is a structured and very useful Problem Solving template. To be successful, this template must be supported by a Lean Culture that changes how we view problems. Otherwise, A3 Team Based Problem Solving will just join the list of "programs of the month."

Error Proofing/Mistake Proofing

Many American organizations believe that processes cannot always be done "right the first time." They have been conditioned to believe that the concept of "zero defects" is impossible or, if it is possible, achieving it will make their projects or services "too expensive."

With Error Proofing, Zero Defects is Possible!

Consequently, a lot of money is spent inspecting, reworking, or redoing things to get them right. In fact, there are companies that believe so strongly that "achieving zero defects" is impossible that they want their customers to inspect the product for them. Figure 4.11 is an example.

CUSTOMER INFORMATION

Although Stamina tries to manufacture its products with the finest materials and using the highest standards of manufacturing, occasionally a defective part is not found in the inspection process. Also, from time to time, a part necessary for operation is not shipped with the product. Even with the highest inspection and quality controls in place these things will happen occasionally.

For your convenience, Stamina has a CUSTOMER SERVICE DEPARTMENT with an 800 number. Should a part be missing or a defective part be found, please call **800-375-7520** (in the U.S.) between 8:30 A.M. and 4:30 P.M. Central time Monday through Friday. Our operators will be able to assist you with your problem immediately and the part will be mailed within 48 hours.

Please DO NOT return the product to the store where it was purchased as they are not able to handle this type of a problem.

We hope that all parts will be present and in perfect condition and none of this will be necessary.

Thank You,
STAMINA PRODUCTS, INC.

Figure 4.11

Organizations need to stop the practice of putting in inspection stations and institutionalizing fancy fixes that communicate to the organization that it is okay not to do things right. See Figure 4.12.

Figure 4.12
Current Practice - Rework Only,
No Problem Root Cause Analysis - No Error Proofing
(Used with permission)

This thinking is compounded in construction, where projects are generally one-offs and the excuse is made that nothing repeats. Like the discussion in Standard Work, some processes do repeat and can be Error Proofed. If we use the Error Proofing technique of "Prevention" (discussion to follow), the part, product, or process is designed so it cannot be assembled or installed wrong—then one-offs can be covered at the Prevention Error Proofing level.

Occasionally, people and machines do make errors or mistakes. The goal of Error Proofing is to prevent these mistakes from turning into information defects or physical project defects that may reach the owner or affect the project cost or delivery. With Lean thinking, organizations understand that they have process problems, not people problems. They stop the practice of attacking people and implement a practice of preventing systemic process problems.

The ultimate goal of Error Proofing is to produce perfect information or physical project quality. While often thought to be a prohibitively expensive way to produce a project, perfect process or project quality is actually the least expensive way to produce. Perfect product quality requires us to follow the Standard Work and "Do It Right The First Time" (DIRTFT) for every step in the process. When Standard Work is combined with Error Proofing as defects are discovered, the waste of scrap, rework, remake, and reassembly are eliminated, and costs are reduced. Ultimately, when every step of the process is done right the first time, the resulting project has the highest quality and the lowest cost.

Error Proofing is most effective when it is implemented as part of the information or physical product or project design process. There are four levels of Error Proofing (listed in decreasing order of effectiveness):

- Prevention—product or process is designed so it cannot be assembled or done wrong.

- Prevention in station—the computer, tooling, or fixturing prevents or "alerts" the person to prevent the process from being done wrong.

- Detection in station—if the person does it wrong, he or she is made aware of it so immediate correction can occur.

- Detection at downstream station—the person's internal customer is able to detect the defect. This internal customer then communicates the need for correction to the originator so the defect can be corrected.

Using Error Proofing in most companies requires a fairly large change in the culture. Today, organizational cultures tend to consciously support "sweeping under the rug" or hiding problems. Associates that raise these issues are often admonished as complainers or whiners. The messenger is shot!

However, in World Class organizations, associates are rewarded when they raise their hand and admit that an error has occurred. Such a moment is seen as an opportunity to improve. In Toyota, as was previously noted, having no problems is a problem. Once a mistake occurs and is identified, a small team gathers and develops a simple, elegant, and inexpensive way to prevent the error from ever recurring. Error Proofing, like the other Lean Tools, focuses on low-cost or no-cost solutions.

Office and Process Cells

The greatest barrier to teamwork in the administrative area of an organization is departmentalization, grouping people by function. This functional arrangement generates visible and invisible barriers to teamwork while creating motion and transportation waste (see Figure 4.13). As was noted in the teamwork section of Chapter 3, these barriers are strengthened when the Leadership Team gives each department a different goal.

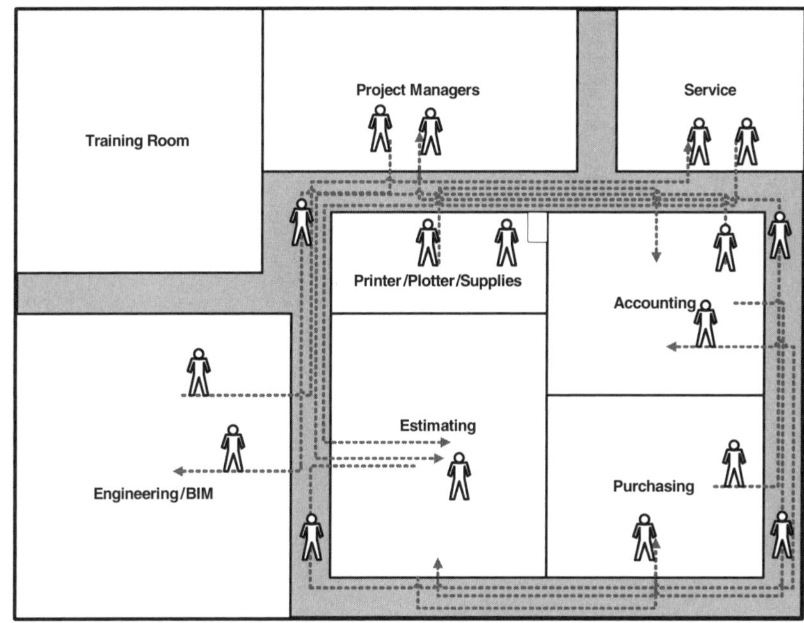

Figure 4.13
Current Practice - Departmentalization

Process cells de-departmentalize people and group them by project, customer, product, or value stream (see Figure 4.14). This approach improves communication and gives the group a common mission and goal(s)—requirements for teamwork to occur. It also reduces transportation and motion waste.

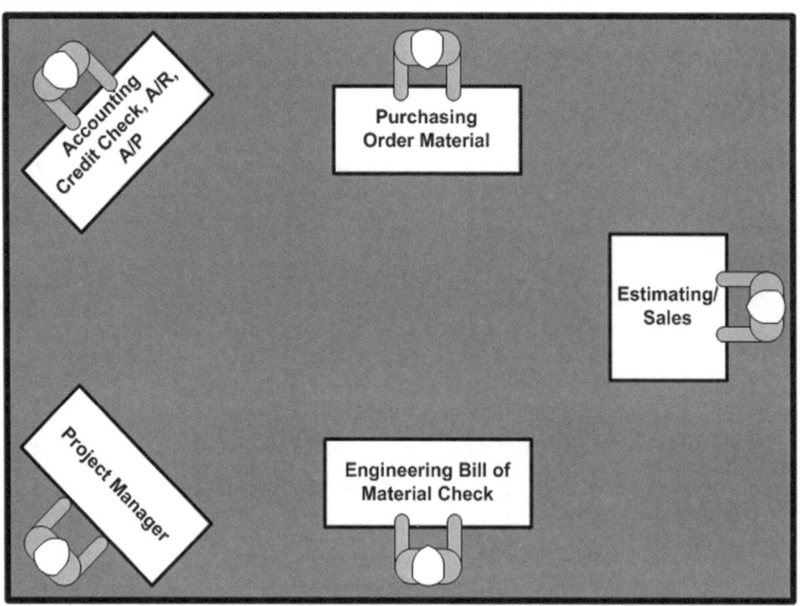

Figure 4.14
Project Release Cell—De-departmentalization

An office or process cell is then a grouping of desks or machines dedicated to the production of a particular information product or physical product. Cells bring together a small team of people who are capable of completing a job or task from start to finish. Cells are formed by grouping together all the people who "touch" a particular information product, or they could just as easily be a grouping of equipment for a construction shop cell or a jobsite prefabrication manufacturing cell. The desks or machines are usually in a "U" shape formation (see Figure 4.14), and the physical material or information packet is passed or moved between desks.

Office or process cells eliminate business waste by

- Reducing or eliminating work-in-process inventory, thereby shortening the process lead time

- Improving quality
- Reducing motion and transportation waste

While improving

- Communication (everyone is close)
- Teamwork (everyone in the cell has a common goal)
- Productivity
- Ability to cross-train associates

These improvements and reductions in waste translate into cellular information or physical product production that is at least 20% more efficient than departmental or functional layout production.

Cells have this impact on productivity, especially in administrative areas, because they help eliminate departmentalization. Departmentalization roadblocks businesses from achieving "Lean as a system" because it traditionally means individual departmental goals. Individual department goals prevent teamwork throughout the organization because everyone is most concerned about achieving their own department's goals. Individual department goals reduce the "system efficiency" because they cause individuals in a department to make bad decisions.

Waste is created when the flow of information stops.

This cell team will become autonomous (if that is part of the organization's desired culture) and thereby can make decisions concerning how they process their work, as long as they are continuously making improvements that support the organization's goals.

Kanbans (kahn-bahn)— Inventory Replenishment System

Kanbans are signals that automate the replenishment of materials and supplies from internal shop suppliers to the jobsite or from external suppliers to the office, shop, prefabrication area, or jobsite using "pull production." The Kanban signal to replenish is sent from the "point of use" (customer) of the supplies or materials to the supplier to pull more materials as they are used. Kanbans place control and responsibility for reordering the supplies and material on the individuals who will be using the materials.

The type of Kanban signal and the replenishment information contained in the signal must be worked out in advance between the customer and supplier. The type of signal used is only limited by one's imagination—fax, e-mail, spot on the floor, empty container, empty truck trailer, Internet, and so on.

Kanbans reduce outages and shortages of materials and supplies, thereby improving the work flow in the office and at the jobsite. Kanbans support "pull project production," continuous flow, and 5S because material is not shipped from the supplier until a signal to replenish is received from the customer's office, shop, or jobsite. Kanbans support the 5Ss because they help prevent jobsite lay down areas from getting jammed with material that may have to be moved many times before installation.

An example of an office Kanban is shown in the following figure:

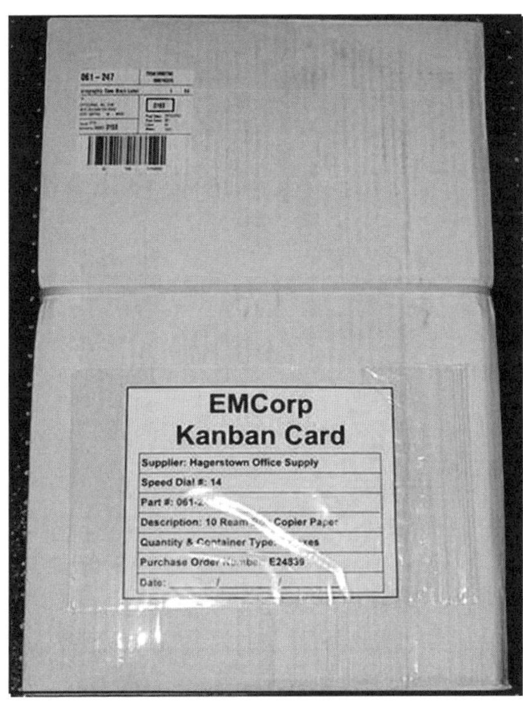

Figure 4.15
Copy Paper Kanban

For this example, the person exposing the copy paper Kanban card is responsible for removing the signal from the card holder and faxing it back to the supplier. The amount of material in the Kanban is generally a one-time calculation based on customer usage and supplier lead times for the material (in this example, how many cases of copy paper the supplier will send back). If either one of these two changes significantly, the amount in the Kanban must be recalculated. Using this approach, Kanbans will reduce overall stock inventory levels (a 30% reduction on average) while eliminating outages that create work flow stoppages.

Kanbans eliminate business waste by

- Reducing work stoppages due to material and supply shortages and outages

- Reducing raw material, work-in-process, and finished goods inventory
- Eliminating overproduction
- Reducing paperwork

While improving

- Work flow
- Project lead times
- Business cash flow

Missing or lost material (including procurement, delivery, and handling) at the jobsite has been and still is the leading cause of jobsite waste and Percent Plan Complete (PPC) reductions. The Electrical Contracting Foundation completed the study in the late '90s shown below.

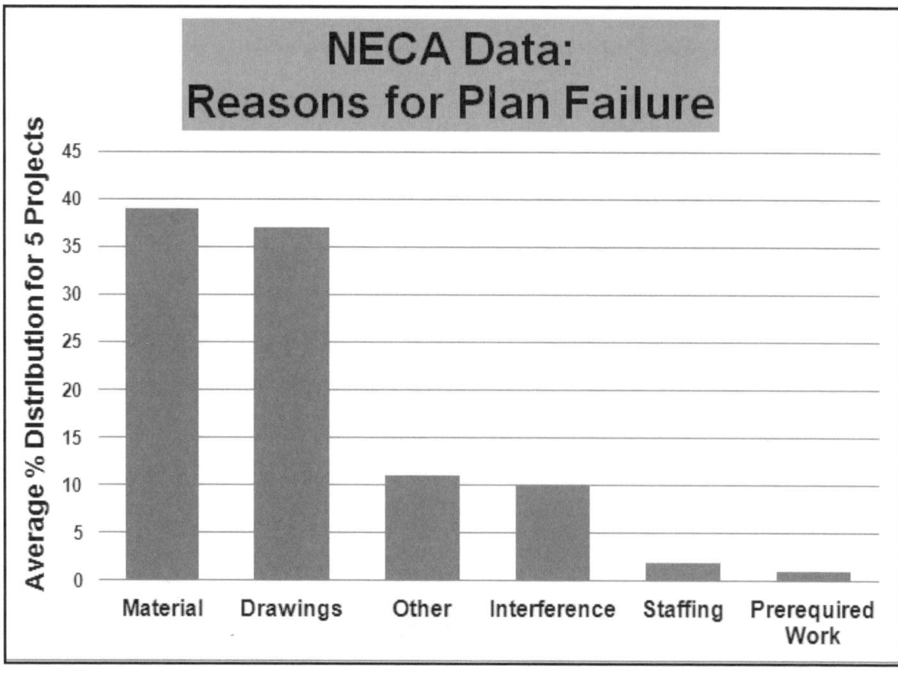

Figure 4.16 Reasons for Construction Plan Failure (Chart recreated with data courtesy of Greg Howell and the Electrical Contracting Foundation)

More recent data from 2011, based on a survey completed by Milwaukee CM, CG Schmidt, confirms that missing and lost material is still the number one jobsite waste. Because one of the roles a Kanban plays in the Lean Tool Box is to eliminate material outages and shortages, this is an ideal application for Kanbans.

A current shop and jobsite inventory replenishment practice that is a variation of a Kanban is called Supplier Managed Inventory. In this system, suppliers come on site to refill stores of high volume, commonly used items such as hardware, piping and plumbing fittings, drywall supplies, electrical system components, and so on. An example is shown below.

Figure 4.17
Supplier Managed Jobsite Inventories
(Courtesy of Grunau Company)

While this technique is far more effective than traditional jobsite purchasing practices, the lack of an actual signal means the supplier may come too often (nothing to replenish) or not often enough (a stock outage occurs). Either "too often" or "not often enough" creates waste.

An enhancement to this technique is the e-mail Kanban, an example of which is shown on the following page. The goal of this system is to put the superintendents and foremen in direct control of material procurement and delivery process.

The foreman would have a set of Kanban e-mails by supplier (covering all supplier materials) stored on their iPhone/iPad/web-capable device application for jobsites. The appropriate supplier can be retrieved in the application via a scan or a search mode. Based on the weekly and daily Lean Project Schedule (see Chapter 5) or during an afternoon and evening walk through of the lay down and supplies areas, the foreman could send e-mail Kanbans to the appropriate suppliers. The gray bars on the signal (Figure 4.18) require the foreman to input information to the supplier that changes as the project progresses. The option to revise the Kanban quantity may reflect defective material or scrap.

An appropriate e-mail confirmation system would confirm the supplier receipt of the signal.

St. Elizabeth's Project
Jobsite Kanban

Supplier: Dortek Door Systems

Customer: Acme Construction

P.O. Number: 11SE—504 (Blanket)

Item P/N: 12704

Description: K Type Single Act. - Insulated GRP

Standard Kanban Quantity: 25 per floor

Project Location: 4557 43rd Street

Required Delivery Date:

Lay Down Area at Jobsite:

Revised Kanban Quantity: (Default = 25)

Figure 4.18
E-mail Jobsite Kanban

Some additional considerations in creating such a Kanban system include the following:

- The use of company-issued electronic equipment to support the application.
- Ease of cancelling, modifying, or adding signals based on product specification changes as the project progresses.
- Limiting access to the application to the person directly responsible for the installation of the material (foreman or superintendent) and purchasing.

Kitting Inventory – Kitting inventory is another potential waste eliminating variation of a Kanban. Kitting creates a portable inventory cache designed to allow the trades to complete a particular activity without making numerous non-value added trips back to the supplies area or gangbox. A plumbing kit is shown below.

Figure 4.19 Jobsite Plumbing Kit (Courtesy of Grunau Company)

Kitting can also be used for more complex jobsite assemblies where it creates both a confirmation that the correct number of parts were supplied and all the parts were used in the assembly. An assembly kit is shown in Figure 4.20

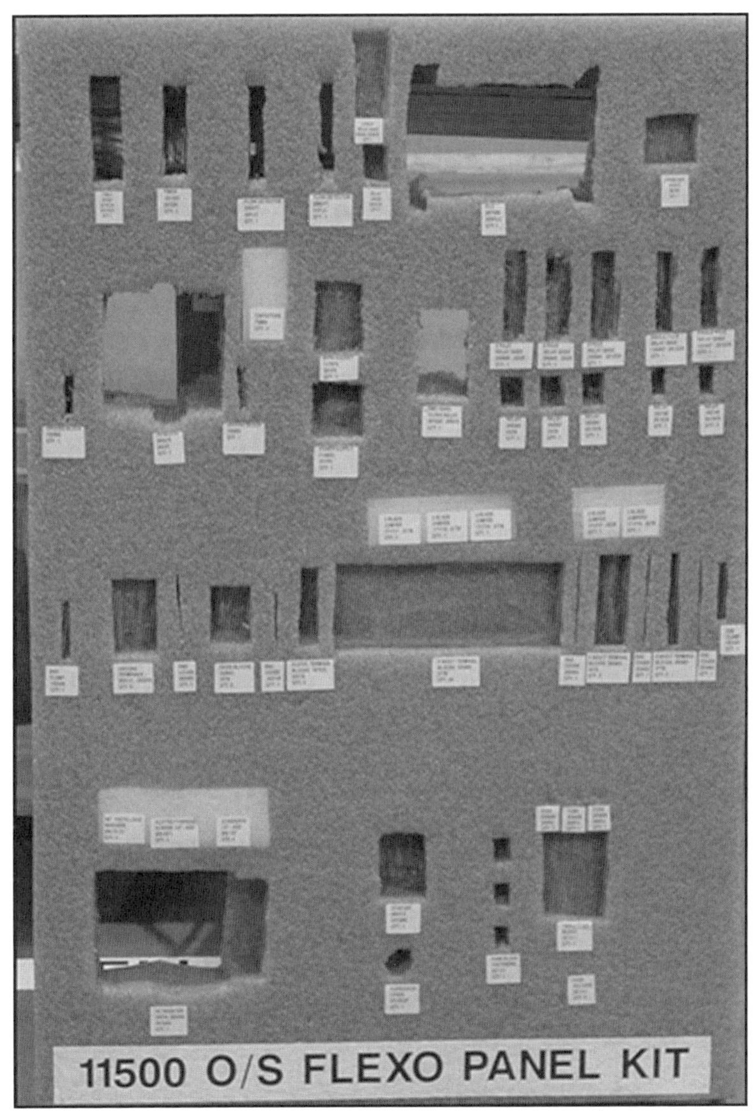

Figure 4.20
Prefabrication or Jobsite Assembly Kit

Consignment Inventory – With consignment inventory, the supplier generally sends material to the customer-specified location, where it sits until the customer needs it. The customer then pays for the material as it is used. While some people call this a Kanban, it is not a Kanban. In fact, it is not even a Lean practice. Lean practices require activities that are win-win in nature. This practice is inventory waste for the supplier, and it has a cost associated with it. Unless this cost is knowingly (by both parties) built into the price of the material, this is not a win-win relationship.

Setup Reduction—Construction Shops

The purpose of equipment Setup Reduction is to increase the manufacturing capacity of current shop equipment while reducing the delivery lead time of construction shop products to the jobsite.

In Lean, setup time is waste because the equipment is not producing materials needed by the jobsite. Equipment value added time occurs only when the machine is changing the "shape or form" of the material.

Setup Reduction eliminates business waste by

- Reducing process lead times
- Reducing scrap and rework

While improving

- Product quality
- Organizational capacity
- Organizational flexibility in responding to changing customer needs
- On-time deliveries to the jobsite

In a machine setup that changes the equipment from running part "A" to part "B," the key to reducing setup time is in understanding these three terms:

- Setup time
- External element of the setup
- Internal element of the setup

Setup time – The time from when a machine stops running the last good part "A" until the time it runs the first good part "B".

External element – That part of the setup that can be completed before the machine stops running the last good part of "A," including gathering up and bringing the following to the machine:

- The "B" drawing and raw material
- The "B" router and job instructions
- The "B" tooling and fixturing

The intent here is for the operator not to have to leave the machine for any reason during the setup process.

Internal element – That part of the setup that can only be accomplished while the machine is shut down—for example, changing the tooling and fixturing (unless the machine has pallet exchange).

Setup time is reduced when all of the current "internal elements" are examined for how they can either be eliminated (as in tooling and fixturing adjustments) or be converted and moved to "external elements."

The target in World Class organizations is to reduce all equipment setup times to less than 10 minutes.

Total Productive Maintenance (TPM) for Shop Equipment, Service Vehicles, and Jobsite Equipment

Total Productive Maintenance (TPM) is a method for continuously improving the effectiveness of all shop equipment, jobsite tools and equipment, and vehicles through the involvement of *all* the people in an organization (not just the maintenance department). This involvement in TPM activities includes the equipment operator, supervision, management, purchasing, engineering, and maintenance.

TPM improves quality, productivity, lead time, and delivery by focusing on improving shop, vehicle, and jobsite equipment uptime and the effectiveness of that uptime.

The goal of TPM is to eliminate all waste associated with equipment, tool, and vehicle "unplanned downtime." Unplanned downtime is waste because it stops the flow of the project or process.

Because no equipment is capable of running 24/7 without maintenance, scheduled or "planned downtime" (when the tools, equipment, or vehicles are not scheduled to be working on a project) is used to keep the equipment running like new.

Definition of Available Maintenance Strategies

- Breakdown – This is the "wait until it breaks and then scramble" or "fire-fighting" strategy. This type of maintenance is also called reactive maintenance. Breakdown maintenance activities are classified under "unplanned downtime."

- Preventative – This is the periodic or scheduled maintenance involving oiling, greasing, adjusting, repairing, or replacing equipment and vehicle components to prevent premature wear and major problems. Preventative maintenance includes overhauls that prevent equipment performance deterioration. Preventative maintenance activities are classified under "planned downtime."

- Predictive – This is the repair or replacement of equipment components or tools before failure based on monitoring equipment operation, historical data, or predicted life cycles. A life cycle can be predicted by

  - Number of completed cycles
  - Operation time (hours, miles, etc.)
  - Calendar time
  - Component wear data (analyzing oil samples, etc.)
  - Variations in the operating parameters of the component such as temperature (electrical equipment) or vibration (bearings)

  Predictive maintenance activities are classified under "planned downtime."

For purposes of this book, the discussion will focus on Preventative Maintenance. Predictive Maintenance strategies start with a discussion with the equipment dealer or manufacturer.

Where to Start an Organization's TPM Activities

It can be very difficult to implement TPM across the entire organization at once, so most companies start their implementation using one or both of the following criteria:

- Expensive tools, equipment, or vehicles for which no back-up equipment or process exists if there is a breakdown

- Tools, equipment, or vehicles that currently have the largest amount of unplanned downtime

Implementation activities start with Preventative Maintenance activities. These activities are developed based on the following criteria:

- The equipment, vehicle, or tool manufacturer's manual of recommended maintenance activities and timing
- The history of previous breakdowns or unplanned downtime
- The operator's experience and recommendations

The developed list of Preventative Maintenance activities is then divided into two sections: activities that can be completed by the user/operator and activities that require a professional maintenance person or dealer. For example, vehicle operators could be expected to do the light maintenance activities of checking and servicing fluid levels, checking tire pressures, and changing air filters. When the vehicle requires a "vehicle lift" into the air to be serviced, then it is taken to the dealer or other professional.

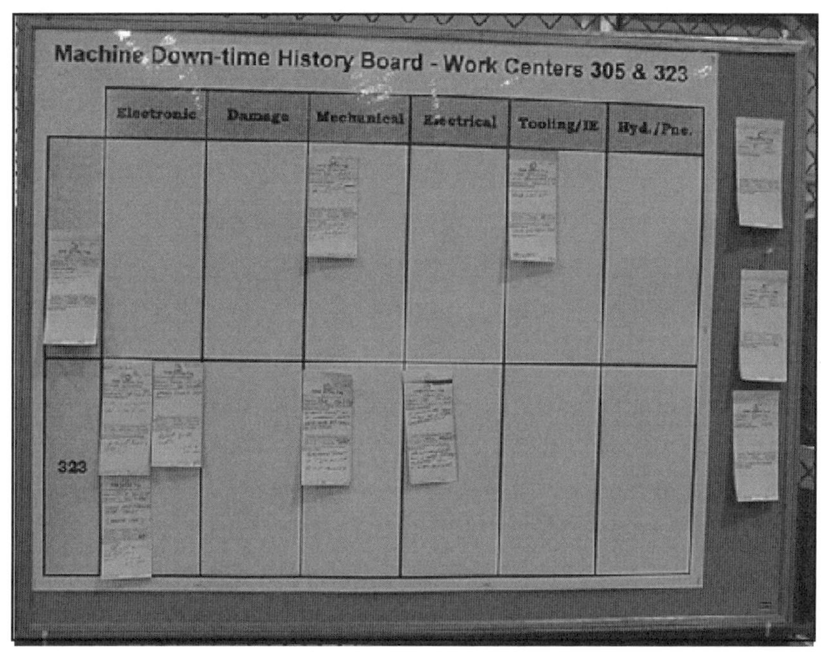

Figure 4.21
History of Equipment Breakdowns

Following this separation of activities between the operator and the professional maintenance people, the remaining items required to start the Preventative Maintenance activities are

- Creating user maintenance instructions—a checklist for these activities with schedules and sign-offs.
- Creating a schedule for dealer or professional maintenance activities. These schedules should be posted clearly in the organization (as shown in the following figure) so people can schedule around this planned downtime.

Figure 4.22
12-Month Preventative Maintenance Schedule

Overall Equipment Effectiveness (OEE) is the key metric of TPM, and it has three elements: uptime of the equipment, the efficiency at which the equipment or tools are running, and the quality of the work coming off the equipment or tools.

Like equipment Setup Reduction, implementing TPM can increase the manufacturing capacity of our current shop equipment by reducing the total amount of downtime (unplanned and planned). Additionally, using TPM to keep equipment in "like new" condition prevents equipment quality and speed performance degradation that occurs over time when equipment is not properly maintained. This like new operating condition will also have a positive impact on the morale of our workforce.

Chapter Summary

The Core Lean Tools, with the exception of Value Stream Mapping, are designed to eliminate identified business waste. The Value Stream Mapping tool is designed to help identify where the waste in a process or system is located. Each tool is designed to target a particular type of business waste.

Because all organizations have hundreds of areas where waste exists, the use of the Lean Tools must be focused to prevent the waste elimination improvements from being random and unconnected to our business objectives. This focus is provided by Policy Deployment (Chapter 2), where all of our Lean activities are focused on achieving the organization's business goals.

References

Fayad, V. and Rubrich, L. (2009) *Policy Deployment and Lean Implementation Planning* (Rev. ed.). Fort Wayne, IN: WCM Associates LLC.

Rother, M. and Shook, J. (2003) *Learning to See.* Cambridge, MA: The Lean Enterprise Institute.

Rubrich, L. and Watson, M. (2004) *Implementing World Class Manufacturing* (2nd ed.). Fort Wayne, IN: WCM Associates LLC.

Sobek, D. and Smalley, A. (2008) *Understanding A3 Thinking.* Boca Raton, FL: Productivity Press.

Chapter 5

The Lean Construction Tools

- Integrated Project Delivery™ (IPD)
- Building Information Modeling (BIM)
- Target Value Design (TVD)
- Choosing By Advantages (CBA)
- Lean Project Scheduling (PS)

This chapter discusses the waste elimination tools that are primarily used in Lean Construction as a result of its “project” orientation.

These tools are active in eliminating waste related to the following:

- Project lead times
- Project change orders related to misunderstood owner requirements
- Scrap and rework
- Waiting and delays
- Lack of a common base of project information
- Lack of Standard Work
- Lack of collaboration
- Lack of teamwork

Because the use of these Lean Construction Tools is accomplished exclusively in a team environment (where the team is generally made up of 4-12 different organizations), team training is required prior to use of tools. Some people have suggested that an effective team process can be learned on the job and during the use of the tool. However, because we were not born team members, this lack of training creates delays, communication problems, misunderstandings, lack of focus, and ill will. All of these and other issues will delay the process longer than the 1½ days of recommended team training. The good news is that the diversity that results from having team members from many organizations will produce a very powerful problem-solving team.

It is also suggested that, after the training, each Lean project team develop Behavioral Expectations or a Code of Conduct for the team that each member of that team signs off on. During the actual project process, this document serves as a reminder of what everyone committed to so they can be held accountable by other team members.

An example of a team code of conduct is shown below:

Project Team Delta - Code of Conduct

1) **Be on time**
2) **Be prepared**
3) **Be committed to the group process**
4) **Listen actively**
5) **Focus on the subject**
6) **Do your fair share and help others**
7) **Be non-judgmental**
8) **Understand cultural differences**
9) **Tolerate disagreements**
10) **Take nothing personally**
11) **Have the courage to ask questions**
12) **Share information**
13) **Treat members as equals**
14) **Work for win-win**
15) **Encourage and support each other**
16) **Commit to team decisions**
17) **Interact with all participants**
18) **Have fun**

"The team solution will be the best solution"

Integrated Project Delivery™ (IPD)

IPD is a project-delivery method with a contractual agreement in which the project risks and rewards are shared between the stakeholders, who are, at a minimum, the owner, the designer, CM/GC, and the principal trade partners.

Project success = stakeholder success.

The goal of this collaboration is to reduce the waste, time, and cost of the project so that the value supplied and owner satisfaction can be improved.

Delivery Approach	Characteristics	Pros	Cons
Design Bid Award	• Two main contracts (design team and contractor) • Best understood • Linear sequence of work (longest delivery)	• Low cost first	• Presents highest risk • Stimulates adversarial relationships • Encourages change orders • Contractor has minimal input in design
Design-Build	• Single contract/responsibility • Faster delivery • Changes traditional roles and relationships between owner, contractor, and designer	• Sole source of accountability • Increases potential for early completion • Less adversarial • Earlier knowledge of firm price	• Minimum innovative design potential • Owner is less involved in design decisions • Owner is pushed for earlier decisions • Not "open book" on pricing and level of quality
Construction Manager (CM-at-Risk)	• Two main contracts (design team and contractor) • Linear sequence of work but accommodates fast-track delivery • CM is selected on qualifications, not price • CM is selected early in delivery process	• Fosters more collaborative environment • Allows for tight control of pricing and schedule • Allows for phased construction • Full disclosure of cost and schedule throughout delivery process • Reduces owner risk	• Perception that price competition is limited • Design team may not take input from CM during design • Still can foster "finger pointing" behavior
Integrated Project Delivery (IPD)	• One integrated form of agreement • Mutual respect and trust • Mutual benefit and reward • Early involvement of all key delivery team members • Early goal definition	• Owner, architect, and contractor act as one • Owner can tailor the best aspects of design-build and CM-at-risk • Shared risk and rewards • Allows for reduction of costs by eliminating redundant efforts • Delivery relationships change from adversarial to collaborative • Increases ability to deliver project within budget and schedule • Increases ability to deliver a more operationally efficient facility	• Perception that cost competitiveness is limited • Can be complex to administer • Can require major culture change on part of the owner, CM, and design team

Figure 5.1
Comparison of Project Delivery Approaches
(Reproduced with permission, Launching a Capital Facility Project)

Why Lean IPD?

Some owners have begun to question the perceived potential cost savings and the amount of delivered value of traditional delivery methods as a result of the following:

- Owners encountering capital restraints and wanting more value
- Owners and Construction Industry desire to eliminate adversarial environments
- Construction Industry desire to share risk
- Construction Industry desire to improve current project delivery processes
- BIM technology supports requirement for collaboration and teamwork

In the book *The Owners Dilemma*, author Barbara White Bryson, an owner representing Rice University, notes:

> As unlikely as it may seem, some owners, especially those in public agencies and legislatures, continue to believe in the value myth of competitive bidding that continues to bog down industry innovation, sentencing us to be eternally locked in inefficient sequential thought, design, and construction processes. Ours is the only trillion dollar industry in the history of the world, in which misguided owners demand processes that increase cost and reduce quality.

"An enlightened owner gets the best project!"

Todd Henderson, AIA
Boulder Associates, Inc.

IPD Prerequisites

IPD is not the right approach for every owner and project. For the project to be successful, the owner must understand, buy into, and provide leadership for what makes IPD beneficial:

- Using Lean as an "operating system" during the planning, design, and construction of the project (using the four components of Lean)
- Using high levels of open, two-way communication to promote teamwork
- Developing teams—eliminating adversarial relationships
- Developing mutual trust and respect (which develops as a result of strong two-way communication)
- Developing mutual rewards and benefits
- Early project goal definition—scope, budget, schedule
- Key project participants who are carefully chosen and involved early (design group, CM/GC, major trade partners)
- Team-based decisionmaking in a shared work space
- Collaborative innovation and cost reductions
- Use of team-based Lean Project Schedule (PS)
- Application of technology (BIM)

Other IPD Barriers

Beyond the owners, key project participants such as the design group, CM/GC, and major trade partners, who all generally work for different companies and have diverse professional areas of expertise, may initially find this team-based decisionmaking environment challenging. These challenges to our thinking and traditional project practices include the following:

- Rather than view the project only as it relates to our company's part of the work, for IPD teamwork and the best project outcome to occur, we must view the project as an entire "system" that is the IPD team's common mission and goal. Like our "system thinking" discussion for the development of Lean organizations on pages 112-113, this requires that all IPD team decisions be made in the best interest of the system—which sometimes may come at the expense of an IPD team member's organization.

- For these system-thinking team decisions to occur, individual team members (for example, the architects) may have to spend more time explaining the thought process and considerations that went into their process of meeting the owner's expectations.

The above considerations make it desirable to select IPD team members from organizations that have a culture and practice of company-wide teamwork, collaboration, trust, and a continuous improvement culture that challenges the status quo.

As was noted earlier, people are not born leaders or team members, so a Lean and Lean team training review is important before starting the IPD process even for organizations with the desired culture and company practices. Without this background, more extensive Lean and Lean team training is required. Additionally, it may be necessary to add a Team Facilitator to an inexperienced IPD team. The facilitator's role is to coach and mentor the team and individual members concerning the team process, help the team resolve conflicts, and keep the team focused on the common mission and goal.

IPD Teams

At least two teams are developed in the beginning: the IPD "Core" team and the IPD "Construction" team. Members of the Core team include the owner, architect/designer, CM/GC (or their representative Project Managers), and any engineers or specialty technology consultants. Decisions are made as a team. The Core team can add other members as it sees fit.

The IPD Construction team is made up of the members who will actually deliver the project, including the CM/GC. The development process map for the teams is shown in the following figure.

Figure 5.2
IPD Core and Construction Team Development

The IPD Process

The major differences between the IPD Process and traditional delivery are the following:

- The project is always viewed from a Lean perspective: how can we drive out "waste" so more value can be provided to the owner?
- IPD attempts to maximize Lean "system thinking." How do we improve the project as a whole? (as opposed to only one system of the project).
- The project is developed concurrently and at multiple levels.
- Knowledge, information, and expertise are shared early and openly.

- Lean "continuous improvement" means the next project will have even less waste (for the same team members).

Using IPD does not guarantee a successful project. With an enlightened owner, it does create a structure in which communication and teamwork are enhanced and can develop into mutual trust, respect, and collaboration. Ultimately, project success is most dependent on the average level of Lean Culture that the individual IPD team members have developed through Lean training and IPD experience.

Building Information Modeling (BIM)

BIM is a process, using both 3-D modeling technology and associated technologies and processes, to create and manage building data throughout the building's design, construction, operation, and management.

The process can produce a model that encompasses building geometry, spatial relationships, geographic information, building materials required, properties of construction components, and quantities required. The Building Information Model that is created then allows for improved communication and collaboration among all the stakeholders in the design and construction of a project.

BIM can supply any or all of the following:

- A potential single source of building information
- Consistent plans, elevations, and section views
- Schedules associated with purchasing materials, fabrication, and delivery schedules for all components, as well as building floor, equipment, and

room schedules (4-D)

- The potential for real-time cost estimating (5-D)
- Shop drawings—i.e., MEP drawings can easily be created when the model is complete
- Interference and collisions can be checked for visually
- Potential for information about the design, purchasing, and construction to be transformed into a record useful to operations and maintenance throughout the lifecycle of the building (6-D)

BIM allows the following:

- Trade partners involved much earlier in the process
- Concurrent reviews with trade partners and suppliers of each of the major elements of the project to reduce the project lead time

Why BIM?

A MEP contractor receives the HVAC contract for a hospital expansion in Hawaii. The ductwork and plumbing will be going from the 3rd floor up to the 4th floor next to the stairs and elevator. A CAD technician draws the ductwork in the most direct route and feels good knowing that he is being efficient with company material. Shop drawings are made, and ductwork rolls out. Plumbing makes a last minute change to shorten the run and also feels good about saving the company money. The plumbing interferes with the ductwork path. A field technician moves the ductwork to fit around the pipes and feels good about problem solving and saving the company work hours. Data systems installation comes in last. Their cable tray can't fit next to the ductwork. Plumbing is reworked. Ductwork is reworked. Deadline is delayed.

BIM—What are the Results of Using It?

- Field productivity improved by 20-30%
- Up to a 7% reduction in project time
- A 10-times reduction in RFIs and change orders
- Clash detection savings up to 10% of the contract value
- Project cost estimation within 3% and cost estimation time reduced by 80%
- Up to a 40% reduction in unbudgeted change.

Figure 5.3
(Stanford University's Center for Integrated Facilities Engineering (CIFE) 2007)

BIM – Barriers to Use

While BIM has been described as the greatest technological advance in the AEC industries in a generation, its adoption and use are still not widespread. The following are barriers to adopting BIM:

- According to the U.S. Bureau of Labor Statistics—68% of all construction firms employ less than 5 people. Their size makes technology investments more difficult.
- Members of the project team of larger organizations who lack IPD and BIM experience may also be reluctant to switch to BIM because of the amount of investment in money and people.
- Resistance to changing from the long-standing definitions of professional responsibility and liability among the project team.

- Some are comfortable with the current iterative design process.

George Elvin author of the book, *Integrated Practice in Architecture*, discusses the advantages of BIM to the project team:

> Because of its comprehensiveness, BIM offers the project team a comprehensive, dynamic, up-to-date model of the project with many advantages over more traditional methods of knowledge representation. It can reduce errors dramatically since information is entered just once, without the need for each discipline to reinput data. And if specific information needs updating, the entire model instantly updates, eliminating questions about which versions are up to or out of date. Because the BIM model is always complete and up to date, coordination between system installers can be greatly improved and workflow can be accelerated. And because team members spend less time on defensive documentation (the phone logs and other records kept in fear of future litigation) and have increased confidence that the documents they are viewing are current, BIM increases team efficiency, productivity, and trust. Increased trust in turn helps build a less adversarial and risk-averse culture on the project. BIM has proven so successful among early adopters that the federal General Services Administration now requires its use on all its projects.

BIM is a rapidly growing, changing, and evolving technological change. Technology providers are rapidly developing add-on applications and solutions to enhance the main BIM applications. However, this rapid growth and change (and the unsettled BIM issues that remain as a result) leave some organizations waiting to make this investment in people and software until the owner requires it.

Still, for the Construction Industry, which is notorious for resistance to change, BIM represents a significant process improvement.

Target Value Design (TVD)

Instead of tabulating costs for a specific design, TVD increases the value delivered to the owner by collaboratively designing to a "detailed estimate" based on a given cost target or the owners "allowable cost." Ultimately, in TVD, the design follows the allowable cost, rather than the cost following the design as in traditional practices.

TVD is a process that requires implementation inside the IPD team model. Owners must be involved in group discussions that establish a team understanding of the following:

- The value required by the owner to establish the basis of the design
- The allowable cost for the stated value
- The schedule

Once the owner's expectations are established, the TVD process requires rapid and frequent communication between the designers and construction contractors, working collaboratively as a team, to establish that the "expected cost" will be less than or equal to the allowable cost.

TVD also produces a cross-training environment in which the designers can learn about estimating and the contractors can learn about designing—increasing the skill levels of both groups.

TVD - How is it Lean?

TVD is a process that

- Creates a common financial goal that supports teamwork
- Attempts to identify and eliminate the waste created anywhere in the current design/estimate/redesign process
- Uses the Kaizen Event brainstorming capability of a cross-functional team to innovate new ideas, designs, and alternatives
- Allows teams to evaluate alternatives using Lean "Standard Work" for the decisionmaking process—Choosing By Advantages (discussed in the next section starting on page 207)
- Can be combined with a Core Lean Tool— Value Stream Mapping (VSM)—to increase its effectiveness

The Lean TVD Opportunities Universe - 30 Year Building Costs

While TVD is typically used to achieve the owner's required value and allowable cost for the construction project, Lean TVD has the capability to impact all aspects of the owner's building costs.

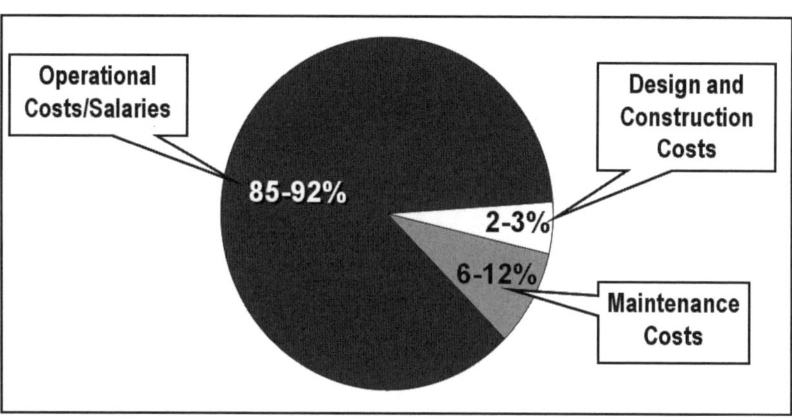

Figure 5.4
Typical Owner's 30 Year Building Costs

Lean TVD Kaizen Events, conducted with members of the Core team and the users, can be used to impact future staffing levels by developing the best facility layout with the least amount of motion and transportation waste (this is especially important in healthcare). Sometimes called 2P (Process Preparation) or 3P (Production Process Preparation), these events can include layout simulations and spaghetti diagrams (maps of the distance and paths people must follow to complete a process).

Once the facility layout is complete, Kaizen Events can then be completed on the department layouts, for example, the lab area. Again, simulations and spaghetti diagrams should be included. Once the lab area layout is completed, Lean Standard Work for the work flow can be created and staffing levels calculated.

This same Lean thinking and Kaizen Events can be used to reduce maintenance costs. Kaizen Events with the proposed maintenance leadership team should be used to make equipment selections and determine maintenance shop locations. Equipment selections should include the following Lean TPM criterion: equipment selected should be designed for "maintenance prevention" (maintenance is not required—like a car battery) or if maintenance is required, it is easily maintained.

After the maintenance shop locations are selected, a Kaizen Event can be completed on the layout. As noted above, do simulations and spaghetti diagrams during this process. Once the area layout is completed, Lean Standard Work for the work flow can be created and staffing levels calculated.

TVD and Value Stream Mapping (VSM)

Although Lean is not a cost-reduction program (costs are reduced as an outcome of implementing Lean), for some construction projects, the project will not move forward if the detailed estimate is above the owner's allowable cost. At this point, a TVD team is formed and trained and a target cost is defined.

Combining VSM with TVD gives structure to the TVD process, making it definable and repeatable. The combination of TVD and a Costed VSM creates a powerfully structured tool for identifying cost-reduction targets (see Chapter 4 for how to create a Value Stream Map). A Costed VSM differs from a normal VSM in that a cost is applied to each process step in the Current State Map as shown in Figure 5.5.

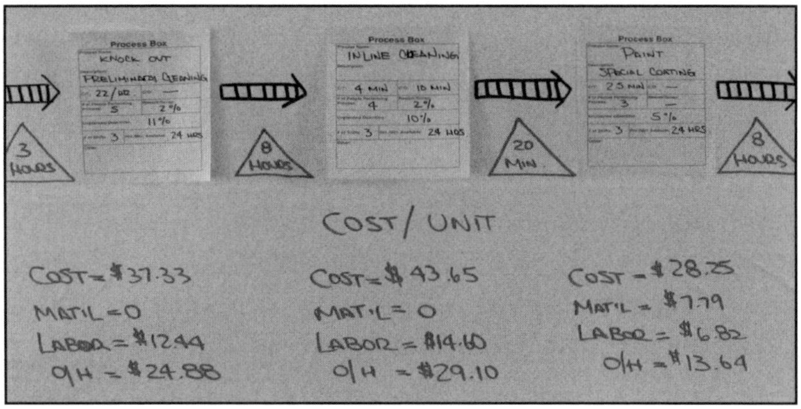

Figure 5.5
Costed Processes

Once the "costed" Current State is completed, the team moves into the brainstorming process. Following the brainstorming rules (page 64-65), the team comes up with ideas that will increase owner value while reducing costs. When the brainstorming is completed, each idea is "cost reduction" valued and "risk rated" by the team based on the following guidelines:

Cost Savings	Risk to Achieving Idea Implementation
1 = Low	1 = Low
3 = Medium	3 = Medium
5 = High	5 = High

This rating of the ideas provides the team members with the information needed to pick the best ideas in the voting process. Obviously, an idea that is rated 5 for cost savings and 1 for risk is an immediate choice.

Using a costed VSM with TVD begins with having a thorough understanding of the owner's expectations and requirements. For large construction projects, it will be necessary to create several levels of maps to limit the size of the maps and to provide details for brainstorming improvements at each level. A large project map breakdown and the staffing for each map might include:

- High level map of the major project components and the flow of work, for example, organized by building envelope, structure, MEP, interior/finishing, vertical transportation, material handling, site improvements, and landscaping. Staffing = Core Team.
- Systems level map. Staffing = CM, GC, trade partners.
- Detail by trade map. Staffing = CM, GC, superintendents, foreman.

A high level map of the major project components could look like Figure 5.6:

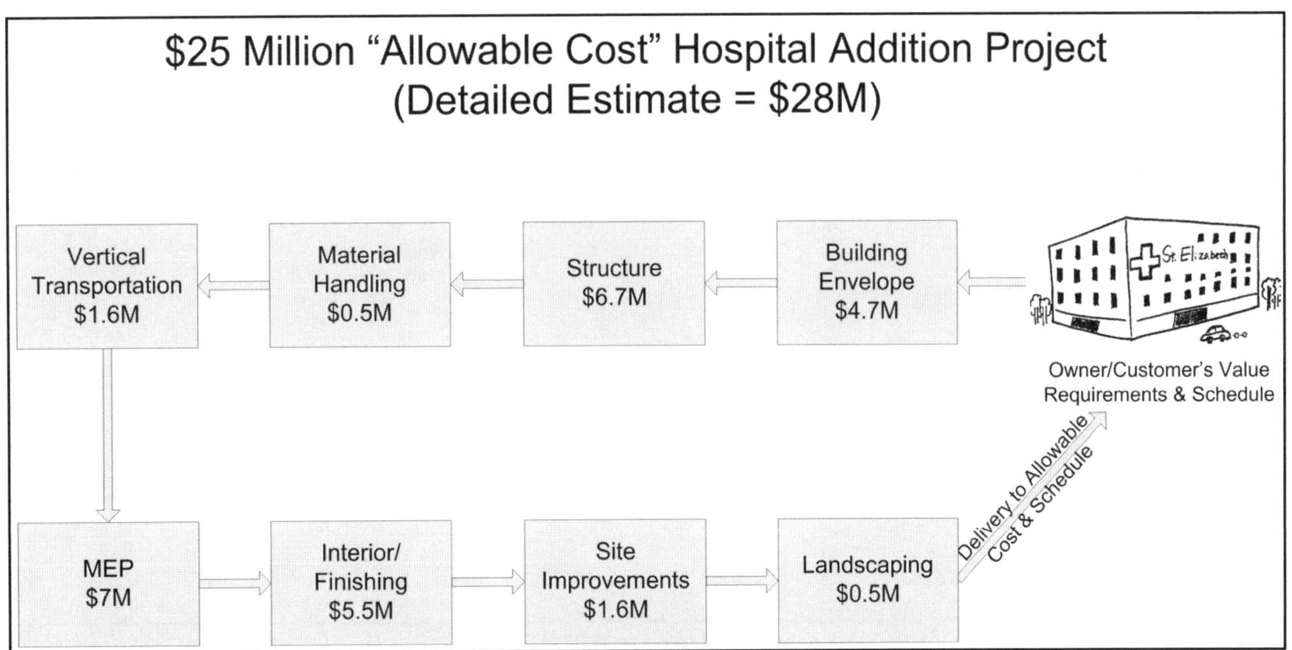

Figure 5.6
High Level Major Components VSM

Because it is difficult and time consuming to investigate all the components for cost reduction, target components for cost reduction can be identified through the following methods:

- Highlighting the highest cost components. Highest cost = greatest opportunity for cost reduction.
- Comparing the component costs from similar previous projects, if available.

In the modified high level map, the highest cost components of the project are highlighted, and previous experiences with similar projects are noted in the box below the highest cost components. An example is shown below:

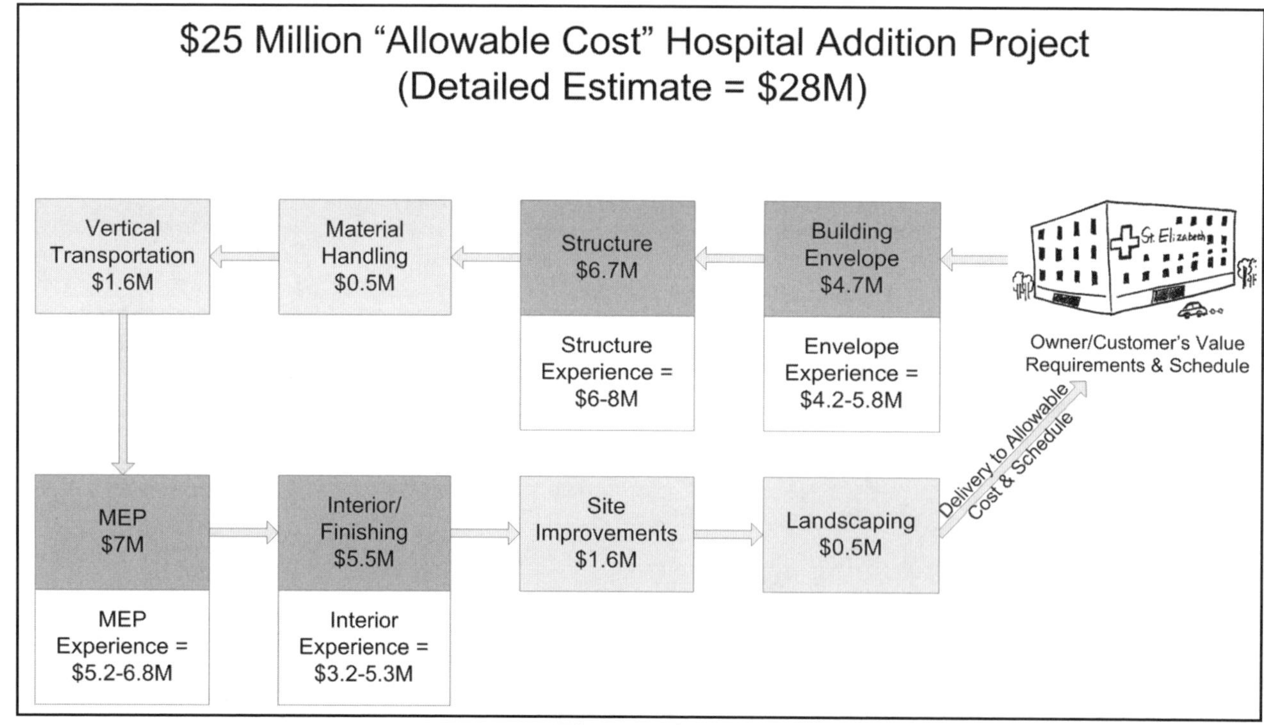

Figure 5.7
High Level VSM with Highest Cost Processes and Experience Noted (Developed in cooperation with CG Schmidt)

Another way to highlight cost reduction opportunities is to compare the owner's value expectations for each of the project's components to the proposed components. An owner's value expectations versus component performance for the Interiors/Finishing component is shown in Figure 5.8.

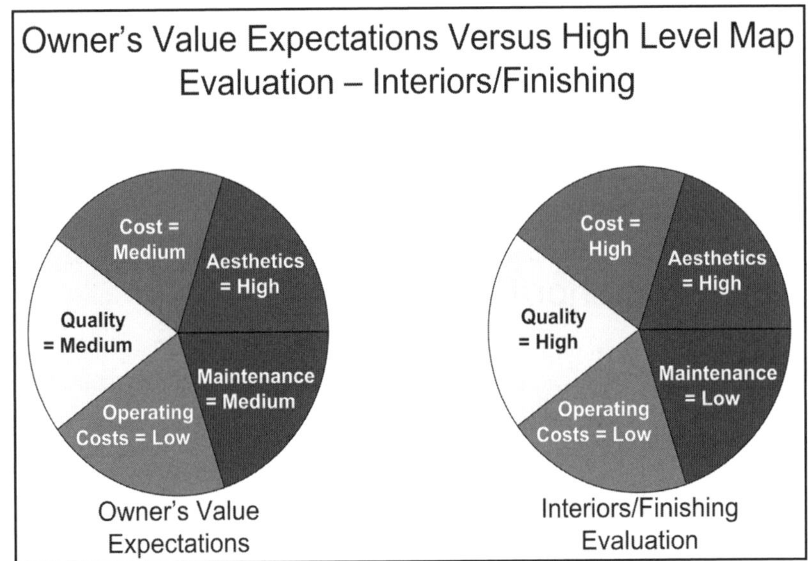

Figure 5.8
Owner's Expectations Versus Interiors/Finishing Evaluation

At this point, the team can follow the standard VSM and Kaizen Event process steps:

- Brainstorm additional solution sets
- Use voting to determine the top three solution sets (if possible), considering interaction effects and lead times
- Use the CBA process (discussed in the next section) to determine the best solution
- Evaluate this change in terms of the allowable cost

The value comparison and VSM/Kaizen Event steps are then completed on the remaining project components that either through experience (MEP) or due to high dollar cost (Building Envelope and Structure) are reduction targets as identified in Figure 5.6.

If additional cost reductions are necessary, the detail shown in the VSMs can be increased by mapping to the next lower level—the system level—or even to the level below that one—the trade level.

The system level VSM for the Interior/Finishing system is shown below.

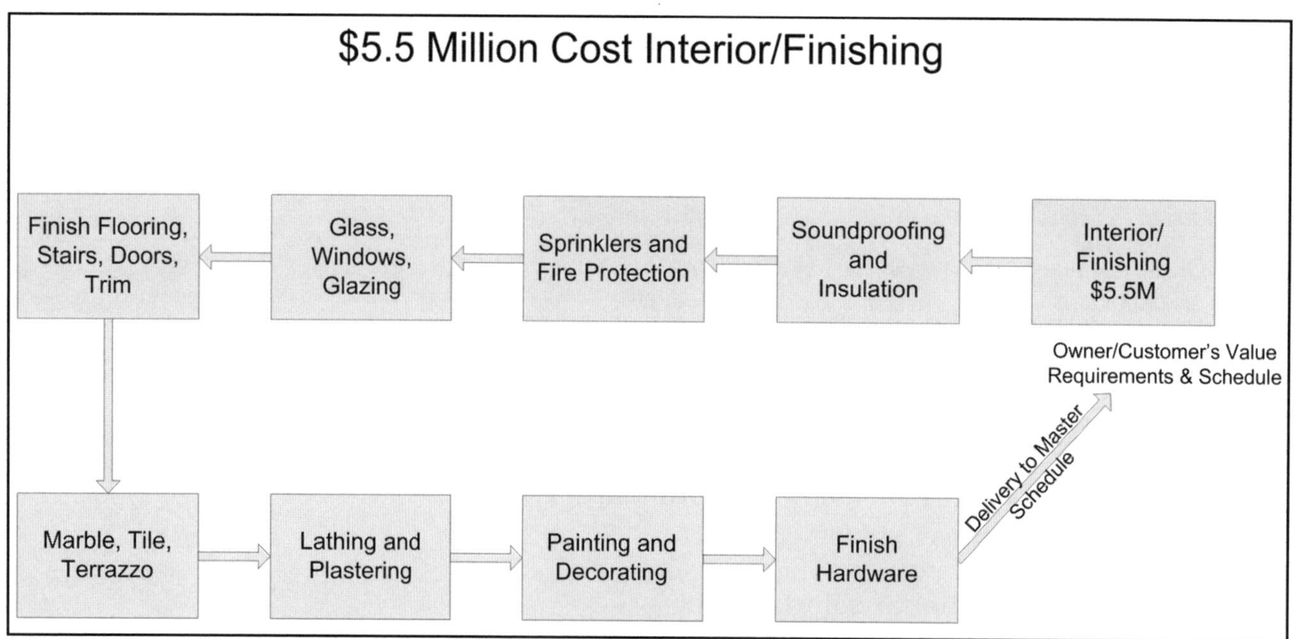

Figure 5.9
System-Level Map for Interior/Finishing

The trade-level installation map for the Terrazzo floors is shown below.

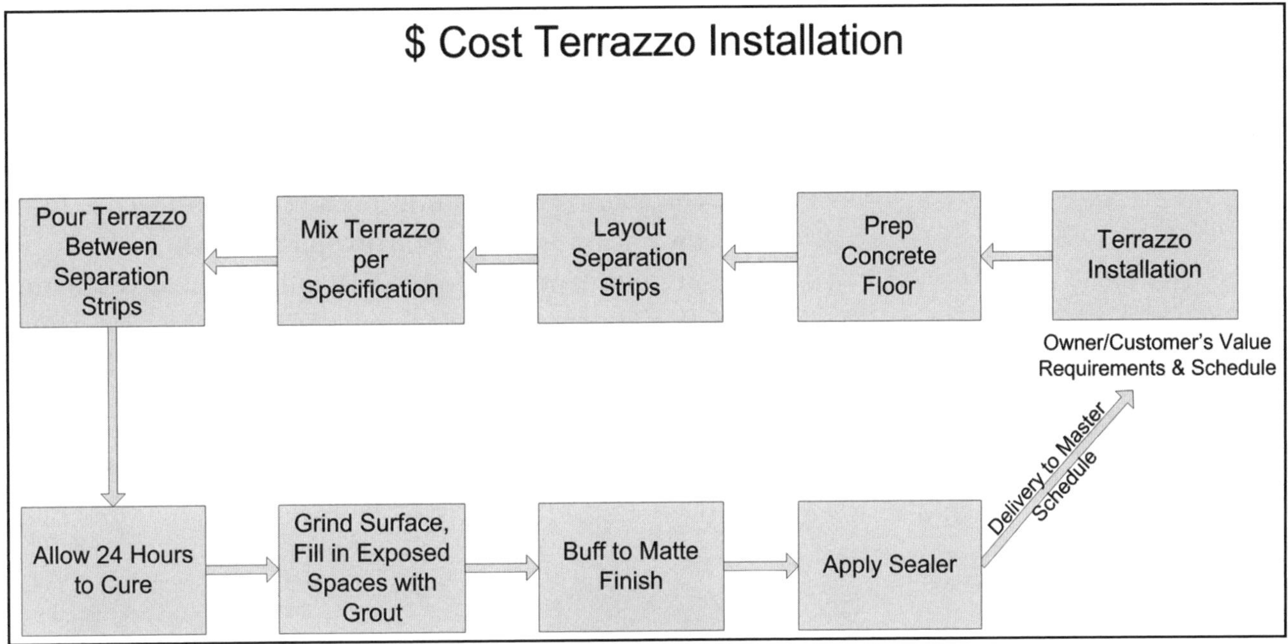

Figure 5.10
VSM Terrazzo Installation

Owner value expectation comparison pie charts are developed for both the high-level and the systems-level maps (system-level pie chart not shown). For the trade-level map, which is developed by the CM/GC, superintendents, and foreman, this value expectation pie comparison is made against contractor developed standards of Lean jobsite practices. For example, on the pie chart shown below, Lean jobsite practices include the following:

- Material lay down area = 30 seconds. This value is derived from the 5Ss. The second S—"straighten"—indicates that if an area is organized, a person should be able to find a needed tool or material in 30 seconds.

- Identified jobsite waste = 0. This element includes a review of the 8 types of business waste and how any of them can affect the jobsite as it is predicted to exist. It also includes a review of the contractor's best jobsite practices.
- Cost overrun = none. This value indicates how the identified waste is predicted to affect the cost as estimated for this project in comparison to previous project costs. Ideally, if Lean continuous improvement is in place, this value is a negative number.

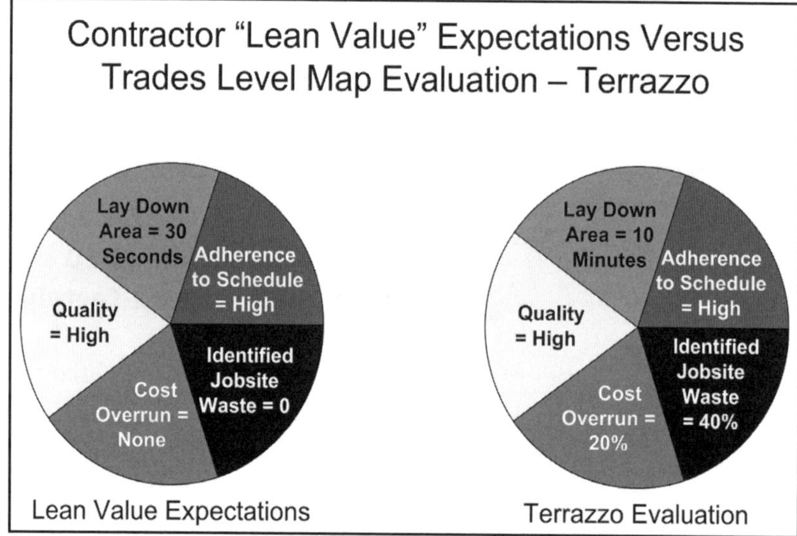

Figure 5.11
Contractor Lean Jobsite Expectations
Terrazzo Installation

Choosing By Advantages (CBA) – Lean "Standard Work" for the Decisionmaking Process

CBA is a *structured* decisionmaking process that starts when a decision must be made and ends when the decision is implemented and the results evaluated. CBA's basic rule of sound decisionmaking is that decisions must be based on the importance of advantages *only*. CBA can "Lean out" the entire decisionmaking process when there is more than one alternative or option.

CBA is often used to evaluate alternatives in a TVD environment, but it can also be used to select trade partners and suppliers (see the trade partners example on page 220). This example and measurement system could be redesigned to allow owners to select their AEC team.

CBA avoids decisions based on

- Gut feel, guesses, personal agendas, and "pet" ideas and suppliers
- Emotion, intuition, unexamined assumptions
- Jumping to solutions, conclusions
- Pros and cons analysis

CBA Leans out the decisionmaking process:

- The diverse Lean team decision is the best decision (a Lean teamwork principle)
- The structured CBA process provides "Standard Work" for the decisionmaking process so that everyone in the organization will use the same format (such as Lean A3 Problem Solving, A3 Reports, and A3 Proposals)

- People who participate in the decisionmaking process are more committed to its successful implementation (a Lean Kaizen Event principle)
- Decisions are documented for reference during the project and for continuous improvement

CBA has seven decisionmaking methods based on the complexity of the decision. The list below shows the CBA methods in order of complexity (simple decisions = Instant CBA, complex decisions = Tabular method).

1. Instant CBA
2. Recognition-Response process
3. Simplified two-list method
4. Simplified tabular method
5. Two-list method
6. Tabular method
7. Money decision methods (not covered in this book—see Jim Suhr's CBA reference at the end of this chapter)

Each of the CBA methods follows six similar steps; however, as the method becomes more capable of handling complexity, the individual steps become more complex. The six similar steps in CBA are the following:

1. A decision needs to be made—**must** and **want criteria** are developed.
2. A decisionmaking team creates a list of alternatives and identifies their **attributes.**
3. The **attributes** (characteristics) of each alternative are summarized.
4. The team determines the **advantages** of each alternative.

5. The team determines the **importance** of each advantage.
6. The team determines the alternative with the **greatest total importance of advantages.**

Terms used in CBA

Criterion - is an instruction, guideline, measure, or rule for the decisionmaking process. Decisionmaking criteria come in two formats:

- **Must Criterion** - an attribute that the alternative must have. Without it, the alternative is eliminated as a potential alternative. In our car example, a must criterion might be all-wheel drive. All cars without this capability would be excluded in step 2—creating a list of alternatives.
- **Want Criterion** - an attribute that the decisionmaking team prefers in an alternative. In our car example, a want criterion might be the highest gas mileage.

Criteria are developed in CBA step 1 and are used to exclude alternatives in step 2.

Alternatives - the decision options that remain after we have applied our criteria (both must and want) to the available choices from our original proposal. For example, if the original proposal is to buy a car, the two alternatives might be Car A and Car B.

Attribute - a characteristic, feature, or distinction (of possibly many) of one of the alternative decisions. In our car example, an *attribute* would be 2 or 4 doors for each model. Attributes are neither good nor bad, except in comparison to other alternative decision attributes.

Other car attributes include miles per gallon (MPG), horsepower (HP), front- or rear-wheel drive, transmission type, color, and so on.

Advantage - a positive difference between the attributes of two alternatives. In our car example, let's assume car A has an attribute of 35 MPG and car B has an attribute of 25 MPG. If we asked which car has the advantage in MPG, the answer would be car A.

CBA Decisionmaking Process Example

The following is an example of the Simplified Two-List Method (number three on the CBA Method's list of seven methods).

This method is used for simple two-option, monetary or nonmonetary decisions, in which the list of advantages per alternative is limited to perhaps no more than four or five. The importance of each advantage can be mentally judged (as opposed to numerical scales that are used and added together in the more complex methods) and the total importance of advantages is mentally decided.

Simplified Two-List Method for Buying a Car

Step 1—Set *must* and *want* criteria:

a) Price must not exceed $30,000
b) Want high miles per gallon (MPG)
c) Want largest towing capacity
d) Want high horsepower (HP)
e) Want high crash-test safety rating
f) Want air bags

For this example, the price criterion must be met, but we will assume both cars have the same total cost.

Steps 2 and 3—A decisionmaking team creates a list of *alternatives* and identifies their *attributes* in order of owner/customer wants.

Car A	*Car B*
• 35 MPG	• 25 MPG
• 3500 lbs towing capacity	• 3200 lbs towing capacity
• 205 HP	• 240 HP
• Frontal offset safety test = Good	• Frontal offset safety test = Good
• Side Impact safety test = Acceptable	• Side Impact safety test = Good
• # of airbags = 7	• # of airbags = 4

Steps 4 and 5—Decide and list the *advantages* of each alternative.

Advantages of Car A	Advantages of Car B
• 10 More MPG • 300 Pounds More Towing Capacity • Three more airbags	• 35 More HP • Better Side Impact Safety Test Results
Total Importance:	Total Importance:
Both Alternatives = Same Price	

Note that the form used to display the data is similar for all CBA Methods. In the Simplified Two-List Method, total importance is a mental judgment versus a calculation that is performed in the methods used for more complex decisions.

Step 6—Choose the alternative based on the greatest *total importance* of the advantages using a mental comparison.

Advantages of Car A	Advantages of Car B
• 10 More MPG (#1 Want Priority) • 300 Pounds More Towing Capacity (#2 Want Priority) • Three more airbags	• 35 More HP • Better Side Impact Safety Test Results
Total Importance:	Total Importance:
Both Alternatives = Same Price	

For the Simplified Two-List Method, numerical ratings for the advantages are not created, and the total importance is not calculated. The decision is made by mental comparison, aided by the order of owner/customer wants. It is interesting to note that, for the data shown, the additional air bags for car A, a "want" criterion, does not improve its safety test results. In this case, the decisionmakers must decide which of the four advantages—MPG, HP, towing capacity, or safety—is the overriding or paramount advantage in this car A or car B decision.

If we add money to the process (car A and car B are different prices), the decision may change.

Step 6—Choose the alternative based on the cost and the greatest *total importance* of the advantages using a mental comparison.

Advantages of Car A	Advantages of Car B
• 10 More MPG (#1 Want Priority) • 300 Pounds More Towing Capacity (#2 Want Priority) • Three more airbags	• 35 More HP • Better Side Impact Safety Test Results
Total Importance:	Total Importance:
Cost: $28,500	Cost: $27,500

If we assumed that the paramount advantage in this decision is towing capacity, then it appears that car A is the sound decision.

To relieve the discomfort we might have about paying the extra $1,000 for car A, we change the comparison to an "equal money" decision. To accomplish this, we must determine whether spending an additional $1,000 on car B could provide additional towing capacity. If spending that additional money produced an additional 500 pounds in towing capacity, car B would be the sound "equal money" decision.

CBA Decisionmaking Process Example - Tabular Method for Buying a Car

The Tabular Method is used for more complex, multi-option, monetary or nonmonetary decisions. It is used when a simplified CBA method does not point to a preferred alternative. The Tabular Method introduces the use of "importance of each advantage" and the "total importance" (this is now a calculation, not a mental judgment).

Step 1—Set *must* and *want* criteria:

a) Price must not exceed $30,000
b) Want high miles per gallon (MPG)
c) Want largest towing capacity
d) Want high horsepower (HP)
e) Want high crash test safety rating
f) Want air bags

Note that these are the same "must" and "want" criteria from the previous Two-List Simplified Method example. Again, wants are listed in owner/customer order.

Steps 2 and 3—A list of alternatives is developed and their attributes identified. The Tabular Method template is then populated.

Factors	Alternatives		
	Car C	Car D	Car E
1) MPG Attribute:	35	32	27
Advantages:			
2) Towing Attribute:	2000 lbs.	3150 lbs.	3150 lbs.
Advantages:			
3) HP Attribute:	215	202	202
Advantages:			
4) Safety Attribute:	Acceptable	Good	Good
Advantages:			
5) Airbags Attribute:	11	11	7
Advantages:			
Total Importance:			
Cost:			

Steps 4 and 5—Start by underlining the least preferred attribute in each factor. Determine the advantages of the remaining attributes and circle the most important advantage.

Factors	Alternatives		
	Car C	Car D	Car E
1) MPG Attribute:	35	32	27
Advantages:	8 More MPG	5 More MPG	
2) Towing Attribute:	2000 lbs.	3150 lbs.	3150 lbs.
Advantages:		1150 lbs. More	1150 lbs. More
3) HP Attribute:	215	202	202
Advantages:	13 More HP		
4) Safety Attribute:	Acceptable	Good	Good
Advantages:		Fewer Injuries	Fewer Injuries
5) Airbags Attribute:	11	11	7
Advantages:	4 More Airbags	4 More Airbags	
Total Importance:			
Cost:			

Step 6—Next, we determine the "weighting" of the most important advantages. Considerations in determining this weighting include the following:

- Understanding the reason, purpose, and conditions surrounding the decision
- Knowing the requirements and "want" preference rank of the customer and/or stakeholders
- Clearly defining attribute magnitudes
- Clearly defining advantage magnitudes

Weighting is a somewhat subjective exercise. It starts with determining the paramount advantage using the challenger-defender strategy.

Challenger-Defender Strategy for Determining Importance Weighting

Make a list of important advantages: 8 more MPG, 1150 lbs more towing capacity, 13 more HP, fewer injuries, 4 more airbags.

Pick one advantage as the defender and one as the challenger and ask the question "Which of the following advantages is the most important one: 8 more MPG or 1150 lbs. more towing capacity?" Answer: 8 more MPG. Having the owner/customer present or firmly knowing your owner/customer or stakeholder preferences is important here.

Continue the defender and challenger questions, "Which of the following advantages is the most important: 8 more MPG or 13 more HP?" Answer: 8 more MPG. Continue this process until only one defender advantage, the paramount advantage, is left (in this example, fewer injuries).

Establish an importance score scale—usually 0-100. The paramount advantage of "fewer injuries" is then assigned a score of 100. The decisionmaking team then weighs the remaining advantages using consensus or the challenger-defender strategy to determine an order for the remaining four most important advantages.

For this example, the importance scale is as follows:

1) Fewer Injuries = 100
2) More MPG = 80
3) HP = 60
4) 1150 lbs. Towing = 20
5) Airbags = 5

The scores are then posted, and a total importance of each alternative calculated. The alternative with the highest value of total importance is then underlined.

Factors	Alternatives					
	Car C		Car D		Car E	
1) MPG Attribute:	35		32		<u>27</u>	
Advantages:	8 More MPG	80	5 More MPG	50		0
2) Towing Attribute:	<u>2000 lbs.</u>		3150 lbs.		3150 lbs.	
Advantages:		0	1150 lbs. More	20	1150 lbs. More	20
3) HP Attribute:	215		<u>202</u>		<u>202</u>	
Advantages:	13 More HP	60		0		0
4) Safety Attribute:	<u>Acceptable</u>		Good		Good	
Advantages:		0	Fewer Injuries	100	Fewer Injuries	100
5) Airbags Attribute:	11		11		<u>7</u>	
Advantages:	4 More Airbags	5	4 More Airbags	5		0
Total Importance:		145		<u>175</u>		120
Cost:						

Note that car D is given a percentage of the importance scale for its MPG being above the "least preferred attribute."

If all costs were equal, car D would be the sound decision. If we add money to the decisionmaking process, the Tabular Method chart looks like the following:

Factors	Alternatives					
	Car C		Car D		Car E	
1) MPG Attribute:	35		32		27	
Advantages:	8 More MPG	80	5 More MPG	50		0
2) Towing Attribute:	2000 lbs.		3150 lbs.		3150 lbs.	
Advantages:		0	1150 lbs. More	20	1150 lbs. More	20
3) HP Attribute:	215		202		202	
Advantages:	13 More HP	60		0		0
4) Safety Attribute:	Acceptable		Good		Good	
Advantages:		0	Fewer Injuries	100	Fewer Injuries	100
5) Airbags Attribute:	11		11		7	
Advantages:	4 More Airbags	5	4 More Airbags	5		0
Total Importance:		145		175		120
Cost:	$28,500		$28,500		$27,500	

Again, to relieve the discomfort we might then feel about paying the extra $1,000 for car D (versus car E), we change the comparison to an "equal money" decision. To accomplish this, we must determine whether spending an additional $1,000 on car E could change the "most important advantage" of any of the attributes. If spending that additional money produced an additional 26 HP, car E would then be the sound "equal money" decision as shown in the following chart:

Factors	Alternatives					
	Car C		Car D		Car E	
1) MPG Attribute:	35		32		<u>27</u>	
Advantages:	8 More MPG	80	5 More MPG	50		0
2) Towing Attribute:	<u>2000 lbs.</u>		3150 lbs.		3150 lbs.	
Advantages:		0	1150 lbs. More	20	1150 lbs. More	20
3) HP Attribute:	215		<u>202</u>		228	
Advantages:	13 More HP	30		0	26 More HP	60
4) Safety Attribute:	<u>Acceptable</u>		Good		Good	
Advantages:		0	Fewer Injuries	100	Fewer Injuries	100
5) Airbags Attribute:	11		11		<u>7</u>	
Advantages:	4 More Airbags	5	4 More Airbags	5		0
Total Importance:		115		175		<u>180</u>
Cost:	$28,500		$28,500		$28,500	

The equal money Tabular Method chart above now shows that car E has the highest total importance score of 180. Note that the total importance score for car C was reduced to 115 because it now has the second level of horsepower advantage at 13 additional HP (as opposed to car E).

CBA Example for a CM Selecting a MEP Trade Partner Using the Tabular Decisionmaking Method

This example is a CM selecting a MEP trade partner from a list of three potential trade partners approved by the owner. The factors used to make the decision will be based on the *Lean Construction Supply Chain Thinking* section of Chapter 6 (page 252). It may be necessary to read this section first to completely understand this example.

In the car buying example, the car manufacture's specifications allowed each car model's attributes to be easily identified. For trade partners and suppliers, a measurement system must be created and data accumulated over time to accurately identify trade partner attributes and avoid decisionmaking that is based only on the bid price, gut feelings, emotions, or personal agendas.

For this example, the trade partner measurement system shown on page 253 will be used.

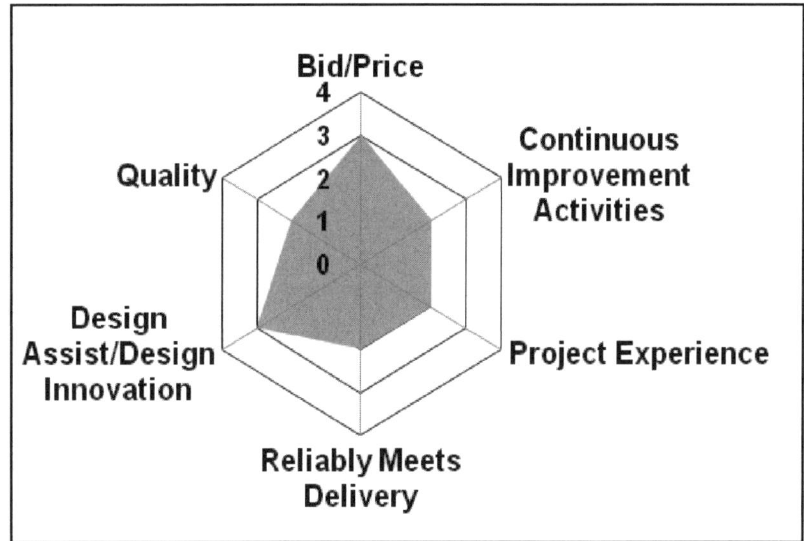

Figure 5.12
Lean Construction Trade Partner Measurements (CBA Factors)

The potential CBA factors for the MEP trade partner as shown in the above figure are as follows:

- Quality
- Design assist, design innovation
- Reliably meets schedule
- Use of CI activities (Lean or Six Sigma)
- Project experience
- Bid/price

Step 1—Set *must* and *want* owner criteria:

a) Bid/price must not exceed $10 million
b) Want Lean processes used throughout the project
c) Want highest quality throughout
d) Want design assist, design innovation capability to reduce final cost by 5%
e) Want schedule met
f) Want similar project experience

Step 2 and 3—A list of alternative MEPs is developed (or, in this case, as created by the "project team" who developed this list using the "must" criterion) and their attributes identified for the five "want" criteria shown above.

The attributes for each trade partner for the want criteria are taken from the measurement sheets developed for each MEP using the following measurement system for each of the listed criteria (Continuous Improvement [CI] and Quality examples are shown in Figures 5.13 and 5.14).

Score (CBA Attributes)	Rating	Rating Details
0	Unacceptable	No CI program in place, no plans of starting one
1	Interim	Organization currently evaluating implementation of CI program
2	Marginal	CI program started, no ideas or contributions yet to organizational process changes that would enhance project value by eliminating waste
3	Good	CI program has produced improved information and material flow on most recent projects
4	Excellent – Partner	Open, two-way communication with a free exchange of ideas and value improvements—both organizations are improved as a result of this win-win relationship

Figure 5.13
Lean Construction Trade Partner and Supplier Measurement Scores – Continuous Improvement (CI) Activities

Score (CBA Attributes)	Rating	Rating Details
0	Unacceptable	Completing the project more important than quality
1	Interim	No previous experience with this sub or supplier
2	Marginal	Occasional rework required, generally passes most inspections and commissioning
3	Good	Done Right the First Time culture. Passes inspections and commissioning on all projects.
4	Excellent – Partner	Done Right the First Time culture. Passes inspections and commissioning on all projects. Uses CI thinking, ideas, and suggested improvements to enhance the quality of the entire project.

Figure 5.14
Lean Construction Trade Partner and Supplier Measurement Scores – Quality

With this information for all five want criteria, the Tabular Method can now be populated as shown below.

Factors	Alternatives		
	MEP "A"	MEP "B"	MEP "C"
1) CI Activities Attribute:	3	3	1
Advantages:			
2) Quality Attribute:	3	4	2
Advantages:			
3) DA/DI = 5% Attribute:	3	4	2
Advantages:			
4) Schedule Attribute:	4	2	2
Advantages:			
5) Experience Attribute:	2	2	4
Advantages:			
Total Importance:			
Bid:			

Steps 4 and 5—Start by underlining the least preferred attribute in each factor. Determine the advantages of the remaining attributes and circle the most important advantage.

Factors	Alternatives		
	MEP "A"	MEP "B"	MEP "C"
1) CI Activities Attribute:	3	3	1
Advantages:	(2 More)	(2 More)	
2) Quality Attribute:	3	4	2
Advantages:	1 More	(2 More)	
3) DA/DI = 5% Attribute:	3	4	2
Advantages:	1 More	(2 More)	
4) Schedule Attribute:	4	2	2
Advantages:	(2 More)		
5) Experience Attribute:	2	2	4
Advantages:			(2 More)
Total Importance:			
Bid:			

Step 6—Next, determine the weighting of the most important advantages. The major consideration in determining this weighting for this example is knowing the requirements and "want" preference rank of the owner.

Remember that weighting is somewhat subjective, and it starts with determining the "paramount advantage" using the challenger-defender strategy.

Challenger-Defender Strategy for Determining Importance Weighting

Make a list of the most important advantages: 2 higher on CI Activities, 2 higher on Quality, 2 higher on Design Assist/Design Innovation, 2 higher on Reliably Meets Schedule, 2 higher on Project Experience

Pick one advantage as the defender and one as the challenger and ask the question "Which of the following advantages is the most important one: 2 higher on CI Activities or 2 higher on Quality?" Answer: 2 higher on Quality. (Again, knowing your owner preferences is important here.)

Continue the defender and challenger questions until only one defender advantage, the paramount advantage, is left: Quality.

Establish an importance score scale—usually 0-100. The paramount advantage of Quality is then assigned a score of 100. The decisionmaking project team, using consensus or the challenger-defender strategy, determines an order for the remaining four most important advantages. For this example, the following importance scale is used:

1) Quality = 100
2) Project Experience = 80
3) DA/DI (5%) = 60
4) CI Activities = 40
5) Schedule = 20

The scores are then posted, and a total importance of each alternative calculated. The alternative with the highest value of total importance is then underlined as shown below. Note that, just like in the car buying example with car D, MEP A is given a percentage (in this case 50%) of the importance scale for its Quality advantage and DA/DI advantage being above the "least preferred attribute."

Factors		Alternatives				
	MEP "A"		MEP "B"		MEP "C"	
1) CI Activities Attribute:	3		3		1	
Advantages:	2 More	40	2 More	40		0
2) Quality Attribute:	3		4		2	
Advantages:	1 More	50	2 More	100		0
3) DA/DI = 5% Attribute:	3		4		2	
Advantages:	1 More	30	2 More	60		0
4) Schedule Attribute:	4		2		2	
Advantages:	2 More	20		0		0
5) Experience Attribute:	2		2		4	
Advantages:		0		0	2 More	80
Total Importance:		140		200		80
Bid:						

For the above importance scale, MEP B is the trade partner of choice. Note the significance and consequences of the importance scale. If the scale is changed based on a change in the owner's preferences to the following

1) Project Experience = 100
2) Schedule = 80
3) DA/DI (5%) = 60
4) Quality = 40
5) CI Activities = 20

with Quality moved from #1 importance to #4, the trade partner of choice, as shown below, would now be MEP A based on the total importance score of 150.

Factors	Alternatives					
	MEP "A"		MEP "B"		MEP "C"	
1) CI Activities Attribute:	3		3		1	
Advantages:	2 More	20	2 More	20		0
2) Quality Attribute:	3		4		2	
Advantages:	1 More	20	2 More	40		0
3) DA/DI = 5% Attribute:	3		4		2	
Advantages:	1 More	30	2 More	60		0
4) Schedule Attribute:	4		2		2	
Advantages:	2 More	80		0		0
5) Experience Attribute:	2		2		4	
Advantages:		0		0	2 More	100
Total Importance:		150		120		100
Bid:						

If the scale is changed as shown below

1) Quality = 100
2) Schedule = 80
3) DA/DI (5%) = 60
4) CI Activities = 40
5) Project Experience = 20

then the total importance score (not shown) would be 200 for both MEP A and MEP B. In this case, the deciding factor could be bid/price.

Just like the structure that A3 Problem Solving provides for the problem solving process, CBA's "template" approach provides structure for the decisionmaking process when there is more than one option.

Lean Project Scheduling (PS)

The purpose of PS is to empower the workforce to work together as a team through frequent two-way project communication. PS empowers the team to take ownership and responsibility for their work, as well as the project's milestones and goals. The communication goals of Project Scheduling include:

- Developing cooperation and teamwork—making sure the needs of other people working at the jobsite are communicated
- Developing win-win relationships by having common goals

The team is also responsible for evaluating the performance of the PS system so improvements can be made.

The result of this empowerment and teamwork will be:

- Reliable work flow (less stopping and starting)
- Less workforce frustration—more workforce control
- Reduced project lead times
- Better quality
- Higher productivity (working smarter not harder!)
- More value supplied to the owner and higher owner satisfaction

PS consists of five components:

1. **Master Schedule**—identifies overall activities, sets milestones, and develops Phase Plans to accomplish these milestones.

2. **Six-Week Schedule**—a look into the future so bottlenecks, limiting factors, and roadblocks can be identified in advance.

3. **Weekly Schedule**—a plan of what will be done (includes "Daily Huddle").

4. **Weekly Scorecard**—reviews what we committed to compared to accomplishments.

5. **Continuous Improvement (CI) Review**—what can we do better in the entire process?

The Master Schedule identifies the overall activities, with durations, for a project, and is usually included in the CM's/GC's original bid. It identifies major project phases and the milestones related to each phase. Additionally, the Master Schedule:

- Places all required activities in sequence
- Gives a complete project work time frame
- Provides duration for all activities
- Identifies long lead time items
- Includes Phase Planning once the project is released

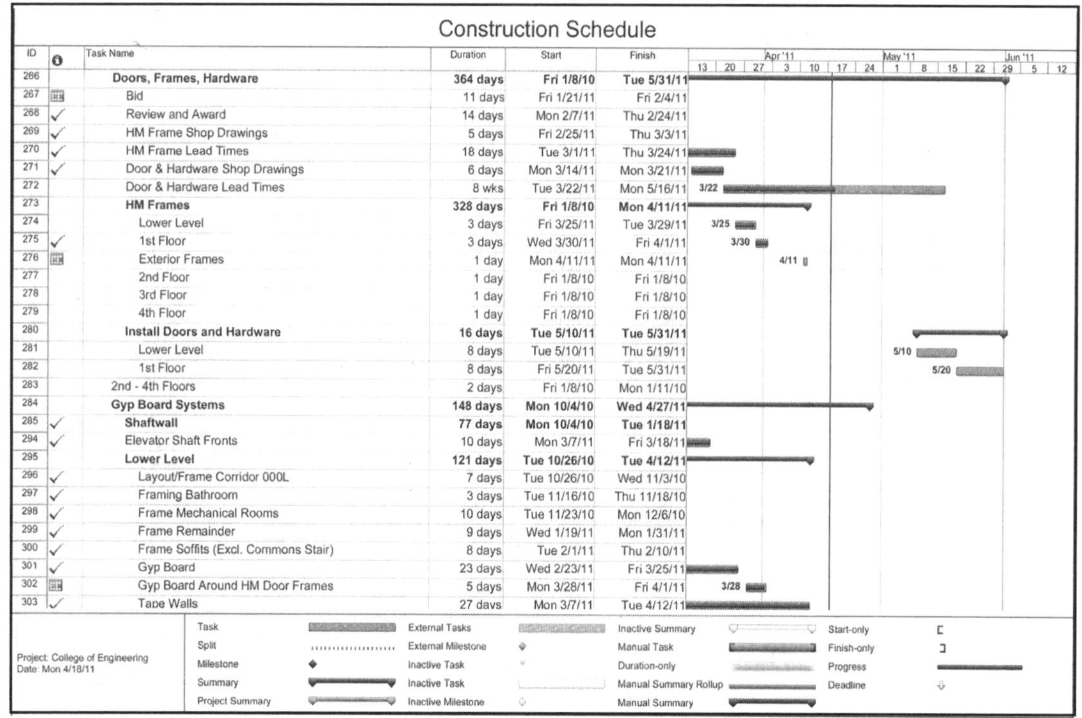

Construction Schedule

ID		Task Name	Duration	Start	Finish
266		**Doors, Frames, Hardware**	**364 days**	**Fri 1/8/10**	**Tue 5/31/11**
267		Bid	11 days	Fri 1/21/11	Fri 2/4/11
268	✓	Review and Award	14 days	Mon 2/7/11	Thu 2/24/11
269	✓	HM Frame Shop Drawings	5 days	Fri 2/25/11	Thu 3/3/11
270	✓	HM Frame Lead Times	18 days	Tue 3/1/11	Thu 3/24/11
271	✓	Door & Hardware Shop Drawings	6 days	Mon 3/14/11	Mon 3/21/11
272		Door & Hardware Lead Times	8 wks	Tue 3/22/11	Mon 5/16/11
273		**HM Frames**	**328 days**	**Fri 1/8/10**	**Mon 4/11/11**
274		Lower Level	3 days	Fri 3/25/11	Tue 3/29/11
275	✓	1st Floor	3 days	Wed 3/30/11	Fri 4/1/11
276		Exterior Frames	1 day	Mon 4/11/11	Mon 4/11/11
277		2nd Floor	1 day	Fri 1/8/10	Fri 1/8/10
278		3rd Floor	1 day	Fri 1/8/10	Fri 1/8/10
279		4th Floor	1 day	Fri 1/8/10	Fri 1/8/10
280		**Install Doors and Hardware**	**16 days**	**Tue 5/10/11**	**Tue 5/31/11**
281		Lower Level	8 days	Tue 5/10/11	Thu 5/19/11
282		1st Floor	8 days	Fri 5/20/11	Tue 5/31/11
283		2nd - 4th Floors	2 days	Fri 1/8/10	Mon 1/11/10
284		**Gyp Board Systems**	**148 days**	**Mon 10/4/10**	**Wed 4/27/11**
285	✓	**Shaftwall**	**77 days**	**Mon 10/4/10**	**Tue 1/18/11**
294	✓	Elevator Shaft Fronts	10 days	Mon 3/7/11	Fri 3/18/11
295		**Lower Level**	**121 days**	**Tue 10/26/10**	**Tue 4/12/11**
296	✓	Layout/Frame Corridor 000L	7 days	Tue 10/26/10	Wed 11/3/10
297	✓	Framing Bathroom	3 days	Tue 11/16/10	Thu 11/18/10
298	✓	Frame Mechanical Rooms	10 days	Tue 11/23/10	Mon 12/6/10
299	✓	Frame Remainder	9 days	Wed 1/19/11	Mon 1/31/11
300	✓	Frame Soffits (Excl. Commons Stair)	8 days	Tue 2/1/11	Thu 2/10/11
301	✓	Gyp Board	23 days	Wed 2/23/11	Fri 3/25/11
302		Gyp Board Around HM Door Frames	5 days	Mon 3/28/11	Fri 4/1/11
303	✓	Tape Walls	27 days	Mon 3/7/11	Tue 4/12/11

Project: College of Engineering
Date: Mon 4/18/11

Figure 5.15 (A)
PS Master Schedule

As Dennis Sowards, President of Quality Support Services, Inc., noted, "To ensure the work can be completed to the milestones once the project begins, Phase Plans are developed from the Master Schedule. Phase Plans are accomplished by starting at the Master Schedule milestones and then working with all the trades in developing a negotiated and iterative 'backwards from the milestone' schedule."

- Phase plans are created collaboratively by the CM/GC and the project manager, superintendent, or foremen representing the trades.
- Provide workforce staffing and duration for all activities.
- Identify hand-off requirements for each activity.

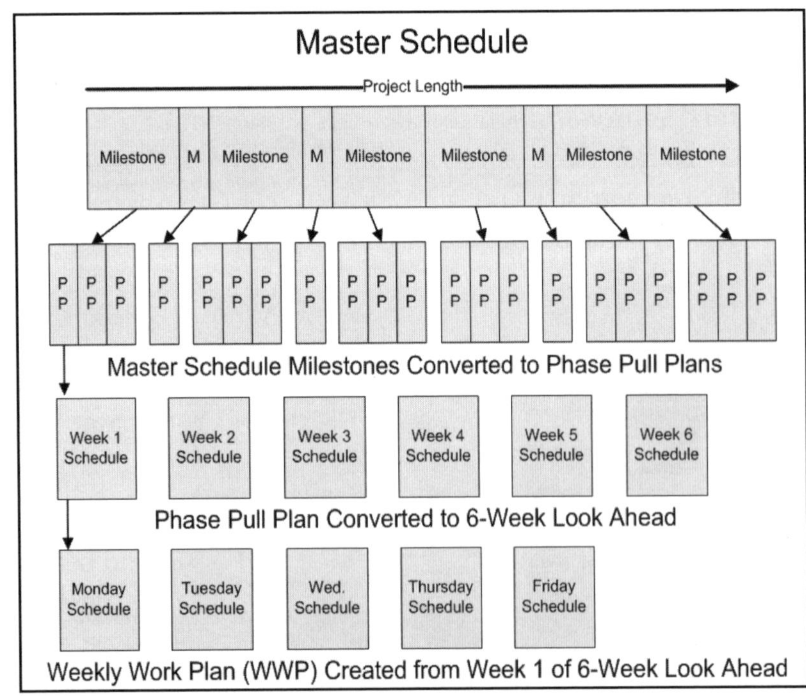

Figure 5.15 (B)
PS Planning Levels

Concerning the Six-Week Schedule, team members meet weekly to look six weeks into the future and review what must be accomplished in accordance with the Master Schedule. This schedule includes the number and type of workers, material, and equipment required to complete the assigned tasks. It is understood and acknowledged that this is the best guess because many things can and do change on a construction project. This "look ahead" is needed to eliminate any "show stopping" roadblocks in the future, as well as to provide necessary information to other support areas within the trade partner or supplier network, such as equipment and materials procurement and shop fabrications.

©GRUNAU COMPANY, INC. Six Week Schedule Project: Hospital											Week of 4/19/2011	
Trade	Area	Repeat	Activity	Responsible Party	Wk 1 4/19	Wk 2 4/26	Wk 3 5/3	Wk 4 5/10	Wk 5 5/17	Wk 6 5/24	Week of 4/19/2011 Explanation of Constraints	Action Required By
PL	1-A		Domestic Water	Kyle +2	X							
SF	1-B		Branches, VAV's, Cond. Traps	Ben +1	X	X						
SF	1-B		B-Mechanical Room	Collin +2	X						Fill-In	
SF	1-C		Complete BB Roughs, Test/Fill	Ben +2	X							
SF	1-E		Dock U.H.'s, MRI FCU, Misc. Trim	Ben +1	X	X	X				Fill-In Work	
SF	1-F		Humidifiers and Steam Filters	Ben +1	X	X						
PL	1-H		Waste and Vent	Kyle +2	X	X	X	X	X	X		
PL	1-H		Domestic Water	Kyle +3	X	X	X	X	X	X		
SF	1-H		Area Build-Out	Ben+3	X	X	X	X			Coord. Drawings	
PL	1-J		Med Gas	James +1	X							
PL	1-J		Finishes	Kyle +2	X							
PL	2-C		Finishes	Dan +1	X							
SM	2-D		Grilles and Diffusers	Mike+1	X	X						

Figure 5.16
PS Six-Week Schedule (Courtesy of Grunau Company)

The Weekly Schedule receives special emphasis. For projects in which many trade partners are involved, the names of these trade partners are entered into the PS. Note that, the Grunau Company Weekly Schedule includes not only the trade assignment, but also the identity of the individuals responsible for the upcoming week's activities. This document creates ownership for all on the project, not just the foreman or superintendent who is responsible for the PS. At the Grunau Company, the PS is not prepared by the Project Manager but by the individual who is actually assigning the work. The Weekly Schedule is certainly more predicable than the six-week look ahead.

©GRUNAU COMPANY, INC.
Weekly Schedule
Project: Hospital

					Week of 4/19/2011						
Trade	Area (Flr-Area)	Repeat	Activity	Responsible Party	Explanation of Constraints	M	T	W	R	F	Action Required By
SM	2-D		Grilles and Diffusers - Install 20 grillles/day, finish installing 2 access doors in return ducts	Justin, Chris				X	X	X	
SM	2-DE		Flip VAV's D218 and E247	Ryan, Lisa, John		X					
SM	2-E		Grilles and Diffusers -Install 20 grillles/day, finish installing 2 access doors in return ducts	Justin, Chris		X	X	X			
SM	3-F		Duct Mains - Cath Labs/Smoke Pure Duct - Measure and send to shop	Ryan, Lisa, John		X					
SM	4-C		Grilles and Diffusers -Install 20 grillles/day, finish installing 2 access doors in return ducts	Justin, Chris		X	X				
SM	4-F		Grilles and Diffusers - Finish last 8	Justin, Chris				X			
SM	4-G		Grilles and Diffusers - Install 18 grills and 7 Anemostats in C-sections	Justin, Chris					X	X	
SM	4-H		Duct Mains - Finish last 4 pieces	Nick, Jim, Scott		X	X	X	X	X	
SF	ROOF		RTU-F Piping - Pipe from floor to first coil	Nathan, Sam, Ethan		X	X	X	X	X	
SF	ROOF		RTU-B Steam Piping - Pipe from condensate trap to 4th floor	Al, Matt, Dan		X	X	X	X	X	
SF	1-B		Branches, 7 VAV's, 7 Cond. traps	Joe, Christine			X	X	X	X	
PL	3-F		Med Gas - Cath lab outlets in north w all, demo existing piping in ceiling, then repipe new in w all	Dave, Lynn				X	X	X	

Figure 5.17
PS Weekly Schedule (Courtesy of Grunau Company)

The Weekly Schedule also includes a daily meeting, the "Daily Huddle." This meeting is to confirm that the Weekly Schedule is on target or to make adjustments that will put the Weekly Schedule back on target. Daily Huddles are normally held at the start of the shift.

To react to problems and issues even faster, Grunau Company has broken its Daily Huddle into four meetings. Taking advantage of the times that the foreman and trades can easily get together, Grunau meets at the start of the shift, at the end of the first break, at the end of lunch, and at the end of the second break.

The fourth aspect of the PS is the Weekly Scorecard. The previous weekly assigned tasks are reviewed to determine what has been completed. A benchmark of 80% of completed weekly tasks is the goal to help ensure that everyone involved takes ownership and assumes accountability for completing their specific assignments for any given week.

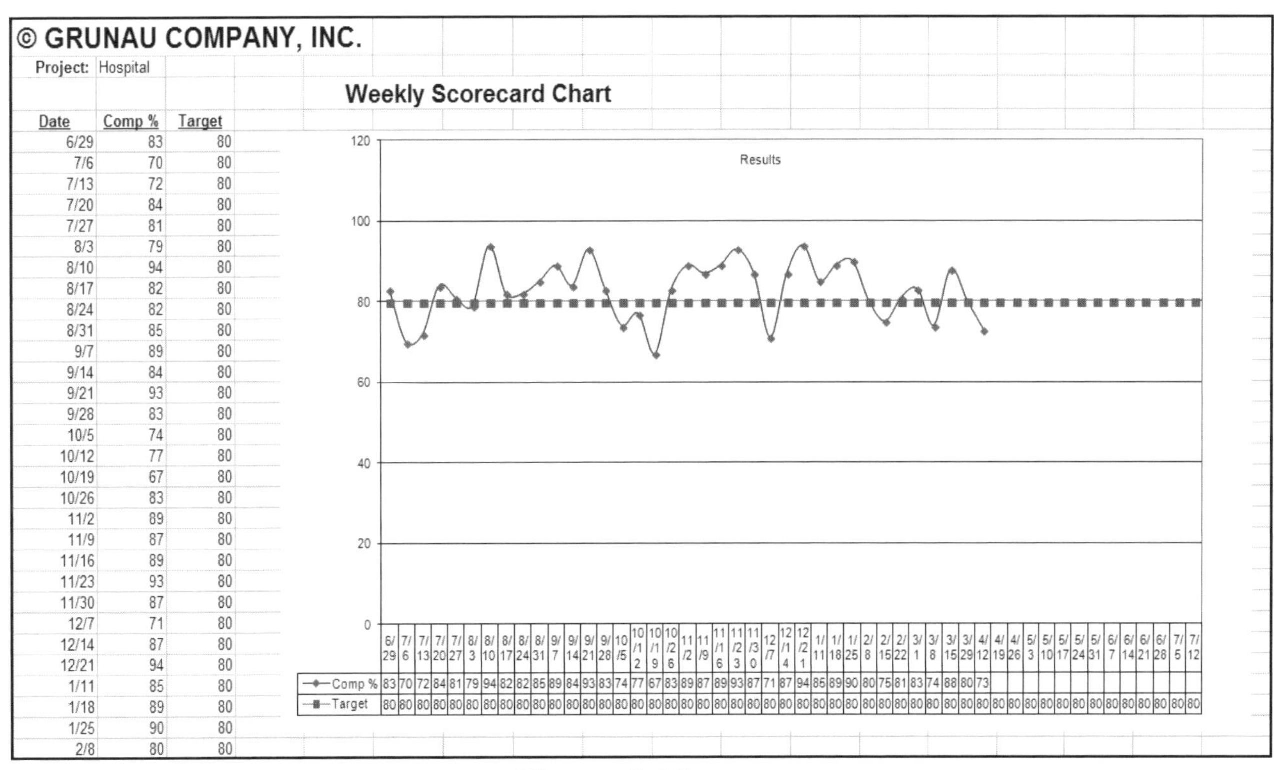
© GRUNAU COMPANY, INC.

Project: Hospital

Date	Comp %	Target
6/29	83	80
7/6	70	80
7/13	72	80
7/20	84	80
7/27	81	80
8/3	79	80
8/10	94	80
8/17	82	80
8/24	82	80
8/31	85	80
9/7	89	80
9/14	84	80
9/21	93	80
9/28	83	80
10/5	74	80
10/12	77	80
10/19	67	80
10/26	83	80
11/2	89	80
11/9	87	80
11/16	89	80
11/23	93	80
11/30	87	80
12/7	71	80
12/14	87	80
12/21	94	80
1/11	85	80
1/18	89	80
1/25	90	80
2/8	80	80

Figure 5.18
PS Weekly Scorecard with 80% as Current CI Goal (Courtesy of Grunau Company)

Continuous Improvement Review is the final part of the PS. Lean is all about continuous improvement, and because no project is currently ever completed "perfectly," this review is an opportunity to make the next project even more successful.

The review should be completed within days of the project completion with as many representatives from the different areas of the organization involved in the project as possible. Typical improvement opportunities that surface in these meetings have their "roots" in communication and teamwork.

An A3 Continuous Improvement (CI) Project Summary Report template (see Figure 5.19) can be used to eliminate these improvement opportunities.

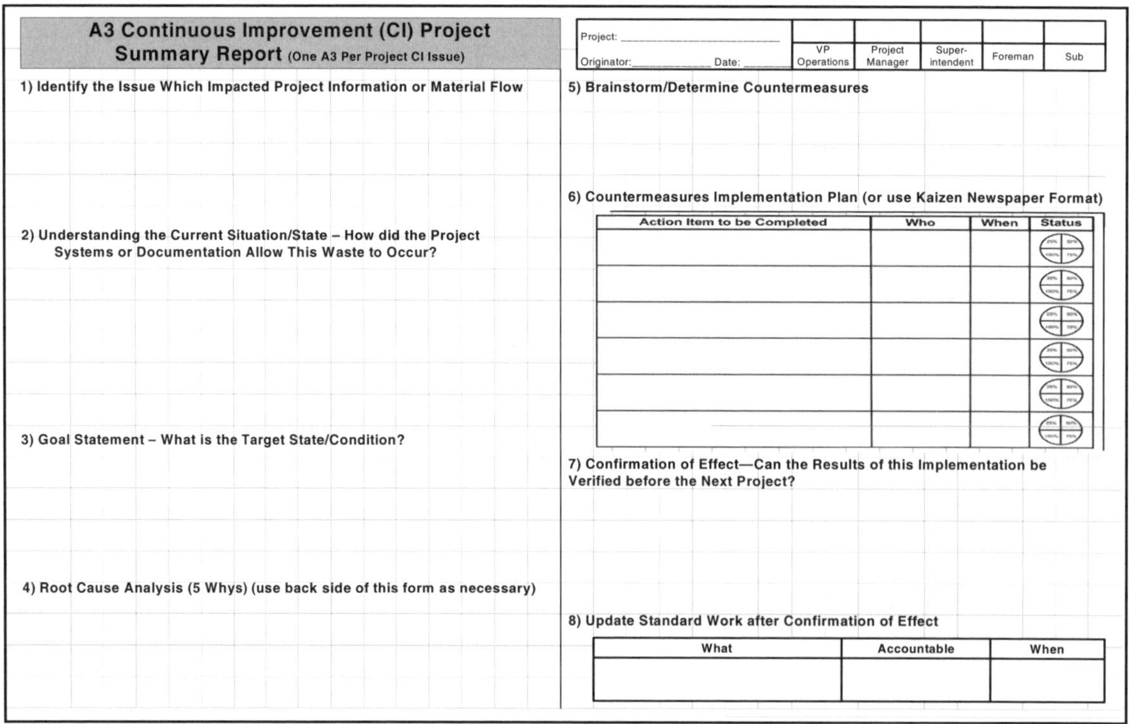

A3 Continuous Improvement (CI) Project Summary Report (One A3 Per Project CI Issue)

Project: ____________

Originator: ________ Date: ______

VP Operations	Project Manager	Super-intendent	Foreman	Sub

1) Identify the Issue Which Impacted Project Information or Material Flow

2) Understanding the Current Situation/State – How did the Project Systems or Documentation Allow This Waste to Occur?

3) Goal Statement – What is the Target State/Condition?

4) Root Cause Analysis (5 Whys) (use back side of this form as necessary)

5) Brainstorm/Determine Countermeasures

6) Countermeasures Implementation Plan (or use Kaizen Newspaper Format)

Action Item to be Completed	Who	When	Status

7) Confirmation of Effect—Can the Results of this Implementation be Verified before the Next Project?

8) Update Standard Work after Confirmation of Effect

What	Accountable	When

Figure 5.19
A3 CI Project Summary Report

All the project improvement opportunities are countermeasured and changed into implementable "action items" whose effect can be confirmed. After confirmation of effect, a plan to communicate the improvements to the rest of the organization must be developed.

An A3 Continuous Improvement (CI) Project Summary Report or an organizational Lean newsletter serves well as an organization-wide communication tool. Action items are normally displayed and tracked using a Kaizen Newspaper format (Figure 5.20) or by posting the A3 CI Project Summary Reports in the area where improvements are taking place.

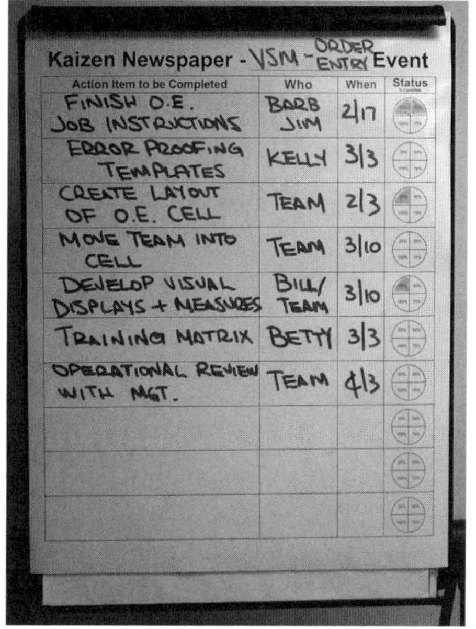
Kaizen Newspaper - VSM - ORDER ENTRY Event

Action Item to be Completed	Who	When	Status
FINISH O.E. JOB INSTRUCTIONS	BARB JIM	2/17	
ERROR PROOFING TEMPLATES	KELLY	3/3	
CREATE LAYOUT OF O.E. CELL	TEAM	2/3	
MOVE TEAM INTO CELL	TEAM	3/10	
DEVELOP VISUAL DISPLAYS + MEASURES	BILL/ TEAM	3/10	
TRAINING MATRIX	BETTY	3/3	
OPERATIONAL REVIEW WITH MGT.	TEAM	4/3	

Figure 5.20
Kaizen Newspaper

Barriers to Using Project Scheduling

Lack of an organization-wide plan

Project Scheduling represents difficult change (and a significant improvement opportunity) for most construction organizations. Without a top-down commitment to both the training and an implementation plan for Project Scheduling throughout the organization, the implementation will be spotty at best. This plan can include using "pilot projects" so that Standard Work (page 142) instructions for using Project Scheduling can be developed for the entire organization.

Lack of jobsite Lean leadership

PMs and Superintendents must change how they run/manage projects from a traditional construction "command and control" environment (always telling people what to do) to a Lean teamwork environment. Using Lean Leadership, we ask the subs and suppliers, as the acknowledged experts at what they do, for their participation, ideas, and commitments to keeping the project on the owner's schedule. We then hold them accountable for their commitments.

PMs and Superintendents must understand the skills of leading the project versus managing the project, and be able to easily switch between them.

Management vs. Leadership Skills

Management:	**Leadership:**
√ Planning & Budgeting	√ Establishing Direction
√ Organizing & Staffing	√ Aligning People
√ Controlling & Solving Problems	√ Motivating & Inspiring
√ Produces Order	√ Produces Change

Lack of Lean Standard Work

Lean Standard Work is the documented procedure for doing a particular process right the first time while minimizing all forms of waste. Standard Work applies to Project Scheduling.

As we noted previously, Standard Work is a difficult concept for the Construction Industry because every project is generally a one-off and all the processes inside the project are broad-brushed with this thinking. However, there are certain processes inside each project that repeat, including Project Scheduling.

While there is some variation in projects that impacts Project Scheduling, such as the length of the project, these variations can be written into the Standard Work. The goal of Standard Work is to prevent ten different PMs and Supers from doing Project Scheduling ten different ways.

Subcontractors not trained

Since subs and suppliers are an integral part of successful Project Scheduling, it is extremely difficult for PMs and Superintendents to do Project Scheduling without the complete participation of subs and suppliers.

Require in your bid/quote package that the subs and suppliers attend Lean Construction training sessions that you will provide prior to the start of the project. This will ensure that everyone is on the same page. The topics for these sessions should include:

- Communication
- Teamwork
- Quality (the goal of no punch lists)
- Project Scheduling and Pull Planning
- Jobsite 5S

Chapter Summary

The Lean Construction Tools are used in a "Lean project-based" environment where two-way communication, collaboration, common project goals, teamwork, a common understanding of the owner's expectations, and a common base of project data among many different organizations is required. This environment allows the waste involved in completing the project to be identified and eliminated, or reduced, while enhancing the amount of value supplied to the owner.

Because many different organizations (with different levels of experience with the Lean project-based environment) are involved in projects, pre-project Lean training is essential.

References

Angelo, T. (2011) *Lean Project Scheduling (PS)*. Lean Construction Newsletter (5th ed.) (http://wcmfg.com)

Bryson, B. and Yetmen, C. (2010) *The Owner's Dilemma: Driving Success and Innovation in the Design and Construction Industry.* Atlanta, GA: Östberg Library of Design Management, Greenway Communications.

Eastman, C. et al. (2011) *BIM Handbook* (2nd ed.) Hoboken, NJ: John Wiley & Sons.

Elvin, G. (2007) *Integrated Practice in Architecture.* Hoboken, NJ: John Wiley & Sons.

Forbes, L. and Ahmed, S. (2011) *Modern Construction: Lean Project Delivery and Integrated Practices.* Boca Raton, FL: CRC Press.

Hardin, B. (2009) *BIM and Construction Management.* Indianapolis, IN: Wiley Publishing, Inc.

Henderson, T. (August 24, 2011) "Target Value Design." PowerPoint Presentation. Boulder Associates.

Kemper, J. (2010) *Launching a Capital Facility Project* (2nd ed.) Chicago, IL: Health Administration Press.

Sowards, D. (2011) "The Complete Master Schedule as Part of Lean Project Scheduling." *Lean Construction Newsletter* (7th ed.) http://wcmfg.com

Suhr, J. (1999) *The Choosing by Advantages Decision-making System.* Westport, CT: Quorum Books.

The Lean Construction Institute. (n.d.) http://leanconstruction.org

Chapter 6

Starting the Lean Construction Journey

"To Improve—You Must Change"

Unknown

Are You Ready to Implement Lean? The Prerequisites for any Type of Organizational Change

In the book, *Leading Change*, noted organizational change expert John Kotter notes that there are five prerequisites to achieving any type of organizational change:

1. Establishing a Sense of Urgency
   - Individuals or organizations do not change without a sense of urgency.
2. Creating the Guiding Coalition
   - Put together a group with enough power to lead and guide the organization through the change. This group should represent a cross section of the organization.
3. Developing a Vision/Mission and Strategy
   - A vision is a broad description or picture of the future state of the organization. Create a vision to help direct the change effort. (This requirement is met through Policy Deployment.)
   - Develop strategies for achieving the vision that include both marketing and operational activities. (This requirement is met through Policy Deployment.)
4. Communicating the Change Vision
   - Use every verbal and visual vehicle possible to constantly communicate the new vision and strategies. (This requirement is met through Policy Deployment during Step 7 enabler activities).

5. Empowering all associates (developed in Lean Culture)
    - Get rid of obstacles that prevent associates from participating.
    - Change systems or structures that prevent associates from creating the change vision.
    - Encourage risk taking and nontraditional ideas, activities, and actions.

Experience has shown that adopting Lean requires, right from the beginning, a strong sense of urgency and commitment from the Leadership Team to the organizational change needed to successfully implement Lean. This commitment to change must include the area in which, generally, the greatest change must occur—the Leadership Team. Without that sense of urgency, the Lean implementation is headed for the "poor return on their Lean investment" barrel of statistics. Prerequisites numbers 2 through 5 are necessary also, but they can be guided and developed in Policy Deployment if number 1 is firmly in place.

The question often asked by managers in organizations is "As middle managers we see the value of Lean, but top management has limited interest. What do we do?" Experience and John Kotter's book indicate how this limited interest can occur:

- Explanations of Lean's organizational impact did not tie into the organization's goals.
    - Why would we want to do this?
- Leadership Team complacency and arrogance (think GM, Chrysler).
    - Lack of a visible crisis

- Have always been profitable, organization screams success. Why change our success formula?
- Too much "happy talk" from the Leadership Team.
- Lack of sufficient feedback from customers and external sources.
- Little tolerance for bad news—a "shoot the messenger" mentality.
- Ingrained strategies and culture that developed over decades are highly resistant to change without a near-death organizational experience (again, think GM, Chrysler).

For the first bullet point, Chapter 2 explained why you want to implement Lean (to create a safe company that makes money) and how to link it directly to the organization's goals.

Unfortunately, successful Lean implementations resulting in becoming World Class only occur when they are "top down." There must be a sense of urgency and compelling business reasons to make these changes throughout the organization. While there have been many attempts at "middle out" and some attempts at "bottom up" Lean implementations, these attempts are more likely to end in the frustration of the attempters rather than meaningful organizational change.

Industry Week (IW) magazine has published, for 21 years, an annual listing of their "Best Plants" in North America. The IW annual award is designed to recognize organizations that are models of improving competitiveness, increasing customer satisfaction, and creating great places to work. Several years ago, the editor of IW was asked whether all these Best Plants had anything in common. His answer—yes, they all had had near-death experiences.

There must be a better way. However, experience shows there is little hope when the barrier to change and implementing Lean is a "brick wall" disguised as most of the members of the Leadership Team.

Is There a Role and Need for Consultants?

The short answer is yes, organizations need consultants, but only to get started on the Lean Construction journey. To be successful with Lean, organizations must ultimately "own" 100% of their Lean activities. Some consultants want to "feed a man a fish" rather than "teach a man to fish" and make the organization entirely independent of them. So choose wisely. Choosing wisely means that, when a consultant is engaged, their exit strategy is also immediately developed.

Ultimately, when properly selected, Lean Construction consultants provide a lot of value and will ensure the organization starts the Lean Construction journey headed in the right direction.

Here are some guidelines for the role of Lean Construction consultants:

- They have "fresh" objective eyes to tell the organization what is really going on in contrast to the Leadership Team's perceptions.
- They will do the initial Lean training, including Policy Deployment.

- They provide guidance on selecting your Lean Construction facilitator (see page 248).
- They will train, coach, and mentor the Lean Facilitator. Their goal is to transfer all their knowledge to the facilitator.
- They will make available all training materials that they use at the company to the facilitator for their use.
- They will train the Lean Facilitator and other selected team members on how to do Kaizen Events.
- They will schedule one-day return visits every 6 months after their exit.

Beware of consultants who:

- Want to postpone the development of an exit strategy
- Do not insist that you need a Lean Facilitator
- Want only to do Kaizen Events
- Do not mention Policy Deployment as one of the first steps in your Lean journey

Do We Need an Organizational Assessment at the Beginning of This Journey?

Any improvement or transformation starts with understanding where the organization is currently at in terms of a leadership, culture, and operational standpoint—the baseline. Very few companies have a good understanding of their baseline. Unless an organization has annual associate surveys conducted by a company outside the organization, the Leadership Team's perceptions and organizational reality are rarely close. Therefore, annual organizational surveys and assessments are valuable tools for associate feedback as a double check on leadership, culture, and operations activities.

Additionally, organizational assessments are extremely valuable to your Lean Construction consultant. They provide an education about the entire organization that allows the consultant to hit the ground running for Lean training and Policy Deployment activities.

An organizational assessment is generally a three-day, on-site activity that develops this baseline by reviewing the status of the following three critical elements of a Lean transformation:

- The Leadership Team and management's readiness to change, support change, and participate in a Lean Implementation. The transformation starts here.
- The current level of associate empowerment and teamwork in the organization (determined by random associate interviews). To become a World Class Enterprise, everyone in the organization must become involved and participate.
- A review and comparison of the organization's current goals with Lean's ability to eliminate waste and improve the organization's processes.

A written report is submitted to the organization with the baseline results and a summary of recommendations.

The Role and Need for a Lean Facilitator

The basic rule is that organizations with more than 100 people require a full-time Lean facilitator. Part-time facilitators work only in smaller organizations. In larger organizations, *part-time* means "no time."

To be clear, the Leadership Team must own the Lean implementation for the organization. The Lean Facilitator is the organization's Lean in-house "expert" (consultant) who supports the rest of the organization in their execution of the deployment plan. Organizationally, the Lean Facilitator is a dotted line or direct report to the top manager in the facility.

As opposed to manufacturing, where a single Lean Facilitator can support a Lean launch in a single 500 person facility (at least during the ramp up), the geographic challenges posed by multiple remote jobsites require additional Lean Leader support at the project level. In construction, the project superintendent best fills this Lean Leader role. The superintendent continues to run the jobsite, but now does it from a Lean Leader perspective.

To prevent the superintendents from getting bogged down with explaining Lean to untrained Lean suppliers and trade partners, the GC/CM must require in the bid package that the suppliers and subs attend Lean Construction training sessions (taught by the Lean Facilitator) that you will provide prior to the start of the project. This will ensure everyone is on the same page from the get-go. Topics for these sessions should include:

- Lean Thinking
- Communication

- Collaboration and Teamwork
- Quality (the goal of no punch lists)
- Project Scheduling and Pull Planning
- Jobsite 5S and Kanbans

From an organizational perspective, the Lean Leader and Lean Facilitator's responsibilities are broken down as follows:

Lean Leader

- Creates and supports an environment of communication, collaboration, and teamwork on the jobsite
- Uses Project Scheduling and Pull Planning to ensure the project stays on schedule
- Considers what Lean jobsite activities should become Lean Standard Work for all projects
- Uses A3 Problem Solving to eliminate chronic project problems
- Supports continuous improvement (CI) in everything they do

Lean Facilitator

- Facilitates all Lean training (until other qualified candidates are developed)
- Facilitates the annual Policy Deployment activity with the Leadership Team
- Implements Lean in the office
- Supports the Lean needs of the Lean Leaders, including training, coaching, and advising
- Facilitates Trade Partner and Supplier Lean training
- Works with the Lean Leaders to create Lean Standard Work for the jobsite

- Facilitates all of the organization's Kaizen Events
- Develops other Lean Facilitators as required

The following is a list of our guidelines for choosing a Certified Lean Facilitator candidate:

- Someone in your organization who is passionate about Lean and wants this job. This is not a position you talk someone into or recruit for.
- The candidate must have good communication and people skills.
- The candidate should be someone who is trusted and has no personal or organizational baggage.
- Going outside the organization to find someone is a very distant second choice.

The above recommendations and guidelines should serve your organization well for the first 2-3 years of the Lean implementation. Ultimately, since Lean is not a cookie-cutter approach, the members in your organization will form and develop their own ideas on their Lean organizational structure. Remember, it's all about continuous improvement.

Suggested Lean Training and Implementation Order

There is no cookie-cutter template for the Lean training and implementation order. No two organizations are alike, especially in their starting point. The following guidelines are typical recommendations that may need to be revised or rearranged based on the organization's Lean exposure, Lean experience, and financial situation. This list does not include completing item number 2 on Kotter's change prerequisite list (guiding coalition) or the meetings and announcements that would be necessary if this was the organization's initial kick-off of a Lean Construction journey.

1. **Management training in the Lean concepts and tools (1½ days)**. Using the knowledge learned in the baseline, a training program is developed for the management staff. This session is usually a one-day *Lean Construction Overview* (Figure 6.1). Because Lean implementation failures in organizations are always a result of management issues, this training must include a review of the book *How to Prevent Lean Implementation Failures ... 10 Reasons Why Failures Occur* (1/2 day).

Typical Lean Construction Overview Session

- Why We are Here—Proof of the Need for Lean Construction
- How are American Businesses doing with their Lean Implementations?
- The Four Components of Lean
- Owner Satisfaction and Waste Elimination
- 8 Types of Construction Waste
- Waste is Usually Disguised in Our Businesses
- Management Change Implementation Prerequisites
- Core Lean Tools
    - 5Ss, Teams, Standard Work, Value Stream Maps, A3 Problem Solving, Error Proofing, Office Cells, Kanbans
    - For Shops: Setup Reduction, Total Productive Maintenance (TPM)
- Lean Construction Tools
    - Integrated Project Delivery™ (IPD), Building Information Modeling (BIM), Target Value Design (TVD), Choosing By Advantages (CBA), Lean Project Scheduling (PS)

Figure 6.1

2. **Train the organization's associates in the Lean concepts and tools (1/2 day).** Everyone in the organization should receive an initial 4-hour *Lean Overview*. While many organization's balk at this training because of the cost and difficulty, these same organizations are not measuring the cost of *not* training these associates in terms of rumors, gossip, bad feelings, and resentment. It is extremely important to get everyone on the same page at the beginning of this culture-changing activity.

   This Lean Overview should occur before the Policy Deployment training because some individuals in this group will be involved in the brainstorming activities in Policy Deployment.

3. **Development of a LPO (Lean Promotion Office).** In the long term, the organization must own its Lean activities; they cannot be owned by some group of consultants. Therefore, in-house Lean experts must be developed from associates already in the organization (going outside the organization is a distant second choice). Candidates for these positions should have the following basic characteristics (no recruiting or talking someone into this job):

   - A passion for Lean
   - Good with people, excellent communicator
   - No baggage (respected by everyone in the organization)

4. **Policy Deployment.** This 10-step, four-to-five day management session integrates the organization's goals with Lean and then plans for the deployment of this system throughout the organization. The ten steps are as follows:

a. Determine mission and behavioral expectations

b. Develop/reiterate organization's goals (Safety, Operating Income, Cash Flow, Revenue, ROIC, etc.)

c. Brainstorm opportunities to achieve goals

d. Define parameters to value opportunities

e. Establish weighting requirements, rate opportunities, and prioritize

f. Conduct a reality check—will the brainstormed ideas achieve the goals?

g. Develop Lean Implementation Plan

h. Cascade company goals into operational metrics and develop Bowling Chart

i. Determine countermeasures—A3 Team Based Problem Solving, Error Proofing, and DMAIC

j. How to conduct monthly Business Reviews—deployment follow up

5. **Begin enabler activities, Value Stream Mapping, and other Kaizen Event activities as identified in the Deployment Plan.**

   - Conduct roll-out activities for the plan that management developed, making sure all the metrics are visual.

6. **Follow-up, review, and adjust on a continuing basis.** This means doing the following:

   a. Conducting monthly Business Reviews

   b. Adjusting your plan as markets and customer requirements change

   c. Making the Policy Deployment activity part of how the organization does business

At the six-month and one-year points in the implementation, the outside consultant should conduct one-day reviews to look for gaps or problems in the completeness of the training or the Lean Implementation Plan, as well as to determine the developmental status of the Lean Facilitator.

In addition, remember that Policy Deployment is an annual process, just like the budgeting process it can usually replace. Start the PD process as early as possible, and for the best PD results, involve as many members of the organization as possible, as noted in Chapter 2.

Lean Construction Supply Chain Thinking

As mentioned in Chapter 2, in Lean Manufacturing, the idea of a Lean Supply Chain is common. Organizations moving toward World Class status understand that they cannot become a World Class organization without World Class suppliers, or put another way, organizations can never be better than their worst supplier. Lean Manufacturing generally measures suppliers in five different areas as shown on the example "radar chart" below:

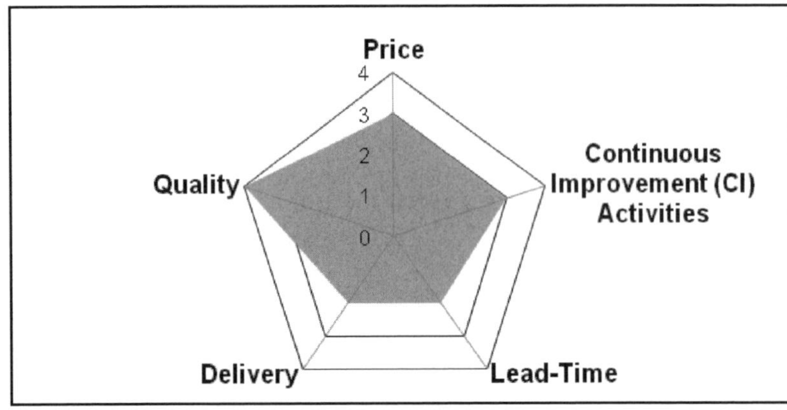

Figure 6.2
Lean Manufacturing Supplier Measurements

Suppliers are selected according to who has the lowest "total acquisition cost" of these five measures. Continuous Improvement activities, like Lean and Six Sigma, are important measures. They indicate that the supplier is trying to eliminate waste so they can improve their amount of value added, meaning they will be able to hold or decrease prices. Often, the selected supplier does not have the lowest piece price.

Ideally, CMs and GCs will use preferred Lean suppliers and trade partners that are measured on "total delivered project cost" rather than just the bid price. A proposed Lean Construction trade partner and supplier radar chart could look like Figure 6.3:

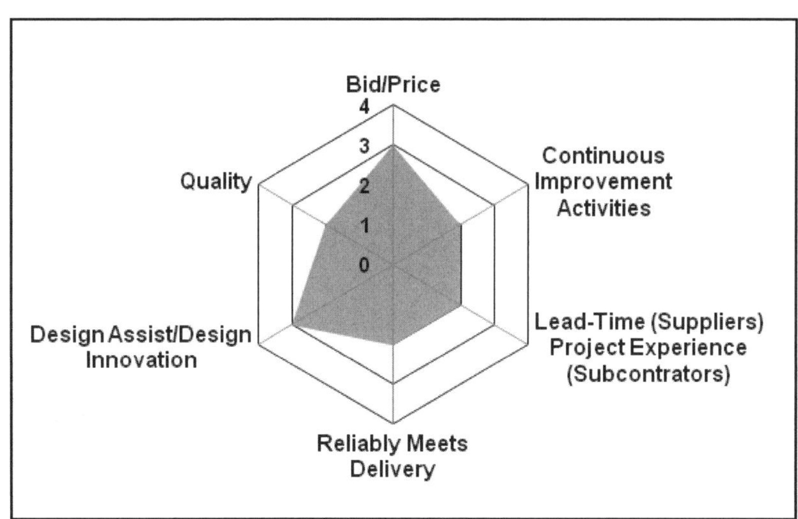

Figure 6.3
Lean Construction Trade Partner and Supplier Measurements

Note that the measurement system for trade partners and suppliers is the same except for "Lead Time" (which applies to suppliers) and "Project Experience" (which applies to subcontractors).

The rating system for each measure looks like the three examples that follow:

Continuous Improvement (CI) Activities: Owners are demanding more value at a lower cost for every project. Meeting this goal means not only identifying and eliminating waste in the trade partner or supplier's operations but also identifying how to improve information and material flow for the entire project.

Score	Rating	Rating Details
0	Unacceptable	No CI program in place, no plans of starting one
1	Interim	Organization currently evaluating implementation of CI program
2	Marginal	CI program started, no ideas or contributions yet to organizational process changes that would enhance project value by eliminating waste
3	Good	CI program has produced improved information and material flow on most recent projects
4	Excellent – Partner	Open, two-way communication with a free exchange of ideas and value improvements—both organizations are improved as a result of this win-win relationship

Figure 6.4
Lean Construction Trade Partner and Supplier Measurement Scores – CI Activities

Quality: Scrap, poor workmanship, and rework can add cost to the project, extend project delivery dates, and reduce owner satisfaction. Suppliers and trade partners must be in the process of developing a "Done Right the First Time" culture that focuses on how their organization can improve their quality outcomes.

Score	Rating	Rating Details
0	Unacceptable	Completing the project more important than quality
1	Interim	No previous experience with this sub or supplier
2	Marginal	Occasional rework required, generally passes most inspections and commissioning
3	Good	Done Right the First Time culture. Passes inspections and commissioning on all projects.
4	Excellent – Partner	Done Right the First Time culture. Passes inspections and commissioning on all projects. Uses CI thinking, ideas, and suggested improvements to enhance the quality of the entire project.

Figure 6.5
Lean Construction Trade Partner and Supplier Measurement Scores – Quality

Reliably Meets Schedule: Owners want projects delivered on schedule. Schedule delays and issues put project quality and delivery at risk. Reliably meeting schedules requires the use of planning tools (like Lean Project Scheduling) and viewing other trade partners and suppliers as team members in completing a successful project as measured by the owner.

Score	Rating	Rating Details
0	Unacceptable	Rarely does what they say they will do—does not use Lean Project Scheduling
1	Interim	No previous experience with this sub or supplier
2	Marginal	Uses Lean Project Scheduling but not effectively. Meets schedules but only after unplanned extra resources are applied toward the end which strains other sub and supplier schedules.
3	Good	Uses Lean Project Scheduling to reliably meet schedules. Coordinates well with other suppliers and subs.
4	Excellent – Partner	Uses Lean Project Scheduling to reliably meet schedules. Coordinates well with other suppliers and subs. Uses CI thinking, ideas, and suggested improvements to enhance the schedule for this and other projects.

Figure 6.6
Lean Construction Trade Partner and Supplier Measurement Scores – Reliably Meets Schedule

The impetus for a Lean Construction Supply Chain must come from as close to the owner in the process as possible. It can be achieved in a Design-Build or IPD environment if the CM or the "core team" recognizes that, to have a World Class project, they must have World Class suppliers and trade partners.

An additional benefit from this trade partner and supplier development program is that the teamwork that develops on a project carries over to and is enhanced on the next project. The flow of information and material is also continuously improved. Projects are no longer a group of "low bid" organizations working together for the first time.

As is the practice in Lean Manufacturing, it is difficult to guide the development of Lean trade partner and suppliers unless Lean is already established in the CM or GC's organization so that their implementation can be used as the model and example.

Chapter Summary

This Chapter highlights the keys to the successful beginning of an organization's Lean Construction journey:

- Top-down leadership and management commitment and support for the changes necessary to implement Lean, including the five prerequisites for organizational change:

    1) Establishing a Sense of Urgency
    2) Creating the Guiding Coalition
    3) Developing a Vision and Strategy
    4) Communicating the Change Vision
    5) Empowering all Associates

- The need and short-term use of outside Lean Construction consultants.
- The value of an organizational assessment at the start of the Lean journey.
- The requirement for the organization to develop it's own in-house Lean Construction expert—the Lean Construction Facilitator.
- How to start the Lean Construction training within the organization.
- How trade partners and suppliers fit in the plan of the organization's goal of becoming a World Class construction organization.

References

Blanchard, D. (2007, October 1) "Census of U.S. Manufacturers - Lean Green and Low Cost." *Industry Week.*

Kotter, J. (1996) *Leading Change.* Boston, MA: Harvard Business Review Press.

Walter, J. *Lean Supplier Development.* Presentation, MarquipWardUnited.

Conclusion

All construction businesses need Lean to survive in the future. The global economic competition, combined with owners demanding more value for their money, requires the industry to improve.

As we noted earlier.

Improvement = Change

So, what are the choices for a new operating system to change and improve your business? We believe that there is only one choice—Lean.

Lean is a powerful, enterprise-wide operating system that can help develop or improve a positive organizational culture while providing a method for annual and strategic business planning (Policy Deployment) and goal achievement. Lean is a sustainable business improvement activity because it recognizes, develops, and uses the resources and capabilities of the entire organization.

Successful Lean implementations are driven by the Leadership Team, which focuses on making Lean the organization's business operating system. Lean becomes the way organizations achieve their business and strategic goals. The development of a Lean Culture creates an entire organization of owner/customer service representatives, working together as a system, trying to provide more value to the owners. It allows the Leadership Team to spend more time leading and developing the future—because they spend less time managing today!

Developing a Lean Culture is a growing and rewarding experience, but what about the financials? From one of our most recent Lean implementations, in 15 months, a facility went from the worst financial performer in a division of 13 companies to the best performer while establishing a facility record of two years without a lost-time accident. These types of results can quickly gain the confidence and full support of even the most skeptical corporate leader.

Lean methods are responsible for dramatic operational improvements in a variety of industries. In addition to construction, typical Lean business improvements include the following:

- Quality improvements
    - From 10% scrap/rework to 0.1%
- Company-wide productivity improvements based on clearly defining owner value and waste – 20-200%
- Reduction in required shop and administrative floor space – 30-50%
- Shop setup time reductions – 70-90%

- Jobsite on-time material deliveries – 99%
- Service lead time reductions – 75%
- Inventory reductions – 75%

In my personal experience as a Lean leader and manager, I have been both challenged and rewarded by the Lean journey spelled out in this book. During the development of the steps involved in this journey, sometimes it was one step forward and then two steps back. Although painful for a Lean thinker, this trial-and-experience approach was necessary when there were no maps. More frustration was provided by corporate "leaders" who always questioned new systems that were not immediately profitable and who were always willing to send "adult help" to change it back to the way it was. Ultimately, though, to see people grow both as individuals and members of the organizations, teamwork develop, and desired improvements occur without management's direct involvement was a tremendously rewarding experience.

Every Lean implementation will have its challenges. The concepts in this book, used as a roadmap, will help overcome those challenges while maximizing the results and rewarding experiences in your journey to become World Class.

Glossary of Terms

5S – 5S is a Core Lean Tool designed to help create a safe, clean, and organized business environment. 5S attacks organizational waste related to

- Injury or lost time accidents due to unsafe work conditions.
- Searching, hunting, or looking for anything—at the jobsite, office, shop, service trucks, computer, or anywhere!

A3 Problem Solving – a structured problem-solving tool that uses a one page (11"X17", tabloid size) template to guide the team through the problem-solving process in an attempt to inhibit the team from jumping from the problem to the solution.

A3 Status Reports and Proposals – The structured template format of the A3 that uses one page (11"X17", tabloid size) is also used for report and proposal writing. A3 Reports are often used in the Target Value Design (TVD) process to document considered project options to prevent the waste of another team spending time with the same considerations.

Behavioral Expectations – a set of rules or standards that members of the organization use to guide their behavior and actions. Behavioral Expectations define the cultural aspects of "how" people do their jobs.

Bowling Chart – a 12-month chart which tracks the results of the Lean Implementation Plan (Kaizen Events) and their impact on the organizational goals.

Building Information Modeling (BIM) – a process using both modeling technology and associated technologies and processes to create and manage building data throughout the building's design, construction, operation, and management. The Building Information Model created then allows for improved communication and collaboration among all the stakeholders in the design and construction of a project.

Business Reviews – The purpose of the Monthly Business Review meetings is to reiterate that the Lean project implementation activities are on target to support achievement of the organization's goals. Business Reviews cover the Lean Implementation Plan and the Bowling Chart. These are Steps 7 and 8 in Policy Deployment.

Choosing By Advantages (CBA) – is Lean "Standard Work" for the decisionmaking process when there is more than one option.

CBA Terms:

Criterion – is an instruction, guideline, measure, or rule for the decisionmaking process. Decisionmaking criteria come in two formats:

- **Must Criterion** – an attribute that the alternative must have or it is eliminated as a potential alternative.
- **Want Criterion** – an attribute that the decisionmaking team prefers in an alternative. In our car example, a want criterion might be highest gas mileage.

Alternatives – represent the decision options that remain after application of the criteria (both must and want) to the available choices from the original proposal.

Attribute – a characteristic, feature, or distinction (one of possibly many) of one of the alternative decisions. In a car buying example, an attribute would specify the number of doors for a model.

Advantage – a positive difference between the attributes of two alternatives. In our car example, if car A has an attribute of 35 MPG and car B has an attribute of 25 MPG, the car with the advantage in MPG would be car A.

- **Most Important Advantage** – the attribute that is most preferred for each factor. A factor is an aspect or piece of the decision (see chart on page 215 for an example).
- **Paramount Advantage** – the factor, as defined by the owner, that has the highest ranking on the importance scale.

Core Lean Tools – the tools that are used in all industries to eliminate the waste that is common to all.

Costed Value Stream Mapping – a Value Stream Map in which costs are added to each step of the process (each process box) so that TVD candidates can be identified earlier and more easily.

Countermeasures – are the Lean and Six Sigma tools that allow the Policy Deployment project team(s) to make autonomous adjustments in their project implementation plan if they discover from their daily measurement system that they are below target.

Culture – is a set of rules and behavioral expectations shared by members of an organization. These rules and expectations produce behaviors within the organization that fall within a range the members consider proper and acceptable. Organizational culture is a learned process and is developed by the organization as a response to the working environment established by the organization's leadership and management team.

Cycle Time – the length of time it takes to complete one step in a process. If the process has four different steps, there would be four different cycle times.

DMAIC – a Six Sigma project methodology—Define, Measure, Analyze, Improve, and Control.

De-departmentalization – the practice of moving people out of departments and into Project Value Streams or into team-based cellular process designs so that teamwork and system thinking are developed.

Empowerment – occurs in an organization when the Leadership Team and management create an organizational environment in which the following occur:

- Associates are recognized as the organization's most valuable resource.
- Teamwork is used throughout the organization.
- Decisionmaking is delegated.
- Openness, initiative, and risk taking are promoted.
- Accountability, credit, responsibility, and ownership are shared. (Here, *ownership* means psychological ownership of the job responsibilities and work area, not stock certificate ownership.)

Error Proofing – based on the understanding that, occasionally, people and machines do make errors or mistakes. The goal of Error Proofing is to prevent these mistakes from turning into information defects or physical project defects that may reach the owner or affect the project cost or delivery.

Guiding Principles – see Behavioral Expectations.

Information Product Production – the "knowledge" or information product is the product produced in the office or administrative area of a construction organization. Information product production includes the creation of models, estimates, specifications, schedules, purchase orders, and so forth, any information required at the jobsite so the "physical" project can be produced.

Integrated Project Delivery™ (IPD) – a project delivery method that has a contractual agreement in which the project risks and rewards are shared between the stakeholders who are, at a minimum, the owner, the designer, CM/GC, and the principal trade partners. Project success = stakeholder success.

Kanbans (kahn-bahn) – signals that automate the replenishment of materials and supplies from internal shop suppliers to the jobsite or from external suppliers to the office, shop, or jobsite using "pull" production. The Kanban signal to replenish is sent from the "point of use" (customer) of the supplies or materials to the supplier to pull more materials as they are used. Kanbans place the control and responsibility for reordering the supplies and material on the individuals who will be using the materials.

Kaizen Events (kai-zen) – also known as "break-through" Kaizen, Kaizen Events are rapid process improvement activities that include the following:

- A team of people (generally 5-12).
  - Associates from the work site.
  - Associates and management people who interface with the work site.
  - Outside eyes (hourly or salaried) – This individual(s) should be unfamiliar with the process and not be afraid to ask questions and challenge current thinking.
- Spending 3-10 days (as required) focused on an organizational process to accomplish a particular Policy Deployment goal.
- The intent to cause rapid, dramatic performance improvement in the process.

Leadership Team – defined here as the top manager in a facility and their direct reports.

Lean Concepts – define the purpose of Lean: the elimination of the 8 types of business waste to improve the flow of both the information product and the physical product.

Lean Construction Tools – the waste elimination tools that are primarily used in Lean Construction as a result of its project orientation. These tools include Integrated Project Delivery™ (IPD), Target Value Design (TVD), and Lean Project Scheduling (PS).

Lean Culture – the foundation on which the Lean implementation can successfully develop. It requires the following elements:

- Leadership
- Communication
- Empowerment
- Teamwork

Lean Implementation Plan – the timeline Step 7 of Policy Deployment that indicates when the selected improvement ideas will be implemented.

Lean Planning – the linking together of the organization's goals and the Lean activities to achieve those goals. This linking is called *Policy Deployment.*

Lean Promotion Office (LPO) – the development of Lean in-house experts so the organization can "own" the Lean implementation.

Lean Tools – When waste has been identified in the organization, the Lean Tools are deployed to eliminate the identified waste.

Lean Project Scheduling (PS) – The purpose of the PS is to empower the workforce to work together as a team through frequent two-way project communication. PS empowers the team to take ownership and responsibility for its work as well as the project's milestones and goals. The communication goals of PS include the following:

- Developing cooperation and teamwork—making sure the needs of other people working at the jobsite are communicated
- Developing win-win relationships through the use of common goals

<u>*Terms Used in PS:*</u>

Master Schedule – identifies overall activities, indicates milestones, and includes developed Phase Plans to accomplish those milestones.

Six-Week Schedule – a look into the future so bottlenecks, limiting factors, and roadblocks can be identified in advance.

Weekly Schedule – a plan of what will be done in a particular week.

Daily Huddle – a daily meeting to confirm the Weekly Schedule is on target or to make adjustments that will put the Weekly Schedule back on target. Daily Huddles are normally accomplished at the start of the shift.

Weekly Scorecard – what was committed to as compared to what was accomplished. Also known as *Percent Plan Complete* (PPC).

Continuous Improvement (CI) Review – asks what can be done better in the entire process.

Manufacturing Cells – see office or process cells.

Mission Statement – a message and picture that can be conveyed to all members of an organization concerning where the organization needs to be and what it needs to look like at some point in the future.

Office or Process Cells – a grouping of desks or machines dedicated to the production of a particular information product or physical product. Cells bring together a small team of people who are capable of completing a job or task from start to finish.

Organizational Assessment – the development of an organizational leadership, culture, and operational baseline so the improvement process has a defined starting point.

Physical Product Production – the physical product created in the shops, prefabrication areas, or at the jobsite.

Percent Plan Complete (PPC) – what was committed to compared to what was accomplished.

Policy Deployment – the 10-Step process to complete the linking of all Lean activities to the achievement of all the organization's business goals.

Reality Check – the step in Policy Deployment (Step 6) in which the impact of the brainstormed ideas is considered in terms of achieving the organization's goals.

Standard Work – the documented procedures and methods for people and equipment, machines, or office equipment to work together and perform value added work while minimizing all forms of process waste.

Standard Work:

- Documents the *safest*, *best*, and *easiest* way to do a job. (The *fastest* way will be an outcome.)
- Focuses on the process procedure (not the person or the outcome).
- Establishes a pattern/routine/habit for the process to be accomplished.
- Establishes a baseline for improvement.
- Makes staffing and scheduling a process or procedure easier.
- Is a living document that changes as improvements are made.

Six Sigma – a business improvement process that focuses on quality advances through the elimination of process variation. Lean, as noted, focuses on eliminating the eight types of waste.

Setup Reduction – The goal of equipment Setup Reduction is to increase the manufacturing capacity of current shop equipment while reducing the delivery lead time of construction shop products or prefabrication areas to the jobsite.

Takt Time – the rate at which a subcontractor's shop or a pre-fabrication area must supply the project's jobsite with material to keep the flow of work moving without delays or stoppages.

Target Value Design (TVD) – used to increase the value delivered to the owner/customer by collaboratively designing to a "detailed estimate" based on a given cost or the owner's "allowable cost." Ultimately, in TVD, the design follows the allowable cost.

Teamwork – everyone pulling in the same direction. For teamwork to occur in any organization, the following four environmental factors must exist:

1) High levels of two-way communication
2) Team members with diverse backgrounds
3) Common purpose/motivated by mission
4) Common goals/measurements

Total Productive Maintenance (TPM) – a method for continuously improving the effectiveness and uptime of all shop equipment, jobsite tools and equipment, and vehicles through the involvement of all the people in an organization (not just the maintenance department).

Value Adding Activity – to be considered as value added, the activity must meet all three of the following requirements:

- It must change the shape or form of the item – for example, creating an architectural model or hanging drywall.
- The owner must care about the activity and be willing to pay for it.
- The activity must be completed correctly the first time—owners are unwilling to pay for rework or repair.

Value Stream Maps (VSM) – the only core Lean tool that will not eliminate waste. Its sole purpose is to help organizations identify the waste preventing them from reaching their organizational goals. Value Stream Mapping creates a one-page picture (although it may be the length of a wall page) of a process, identifying all the steps, sequence, touches, delays, and cycle times for each step of the process.

Visual Communication – part of a great communication program that includes both verbal and visual communication. Good visual communication means that anyone should be able to walk through the organization and understand how everyone is progressing toward their goals without asking a question.

Waste – anything that people in the entire organization do that the owner is unwilling to pay for. Waste adds cost but provides no value to the owner.

Index

Symbols

D

E

F

G

H

I

M

N

O

P

R

S

T

U

V

W